'Son!'

"Wherefore thou art
no more a servant, but a son;
and if a son,
then an heir of God
through Christ."

Galatians 4:7 (KJV)

LIBERATED LIVING MINISTRIES
P.O. Box 98, Roanoke, TX 76262
Tel. 1-800-225-0245
Email: sheasllm@msn.com

Published by:

LIBERATED LIVING MINISTRIES

P.O. Box. 98, Roanoke, TX 76262
Tel. 1-800-225-0245
ISBN 0-620-23413-X

First Edition: 1999 Republic of South Africa
Second Edition: 1999 Colombia

Cover Design by Caryn Poulton

Printed in Colombia
Impreso en Colombia

Contents

Contents

Introduction

"I'm a son! I'm a son!" With the passion and conviction that come from suddenly awakening to a radical, liberating truth, Jerry Smith jumped to his feet, pumped the air with his fist, and shouted over and over again, "I'm a son!"

The other diners in the steak house in Hereford, Texas, where we were eating lunch, were startled by this sudden outburst from this burly custom-harvester from Clovis, New Mexico. Jerry did not care. The powerful reality of the revelation that he had received earlier that morning made him oblivious to their puzzled stares. As the truth exploded in him again with fresh impact, he could not remain silent. Earlier that morning, at Community Church in Hereford, I had taught the truths that are set out in this book. Suddenly, Jerry had jumped out of his seat on the front row and with his big arms, started pumping the air as he shouted, "I'm a son! I'm a son!" Jerry had received the revelation of the same truth that had brought about a cataclysmic change in my life in 1982. I could easily identify with Jerry, whose excitement had caused the sudden outbursts, both in the Church, and, later, in the restaurant.

This book is a description of the change that

occurred in me and is a setting forth of the truths that led to my liberation from living as a servant and entering into the indescribable joy of living as a son. It is unavoidably autobiographical. The transformation in my personal life and public ministry through the revelation of these truths has been so profound that I find myself referring to these events and truths over and over again.

In the years since that time, I have discovered that all too many Christians are living in the same bondage and frustration that I once languished under. It has been my joy to preach these truths and to witness many being set free by the liberating message contained in this book. We have been delighted at the reported impact made through the distribution of cassette tapes that have somehow made their way into many parts of the world. The many testimonies that have filtered back to us have convinced us that among the many precious truths that God has revealed to us and used to liberate His people, this truth should be the subject of the first book that I write.

It is therefore with great delight that I invite you to prayerfully consider the message of these pages. Some of you will find yourselves identifying with many of the personal illustrations. For all of you, I trust that the truths will penetrate deeply into your spirit.

I need to clarify one issue. Throughout the book,

I have, at times, utilized the generic form "son" in referring to a child of God while, at others, I have included "daughter." My motivation in omitting the feminine form has not been sexist, but rather simplicity. The story of the Prodigal Son is at the heart of the message of this book, and so many references and comparisons inevitably refer to the two sons in that story. Please understand "son" in a generic way. I ask, in advance, the forgiveness of any readers who might feel slighted or offended by my choice of it.

It is my bold prayer that not one reader will be able to come to the end of this book and remain in confusion concerning their position in Christ as a son or daughter and an heir of God. The price that the Father paid for your redemption to be a son and daughter is too great for you to continue in the mistaken idea that you have been "saved to serve." May none who reads this book still be in the *"far country"* by the time they complete it. Furthermore, I pray that not one reader will continue living in the servant's quarters, but will assume their rightful place sitting at the Father's table as a son or a daughter, enjoying all the blessings and benefits that are his or hers as an heir. Listen! Hear the Father calling you, ***"Son!"***

John Sheasby
Roanoke, Texas

CHAPTER 1

The Long Journey Home

"Much more those who receive abundance of grace and of the gift of righteousness will reign in life through the one, Jesus Christ."

Romans 5:17

"The way to reign is to receive!" Those were the simple words preached at a businessmen's-fellowship meeting in 1981 that started my search into understanding sonship. At the time, I was pastoring a church in Gweru, Zimbabwe. I knew that God was calling me out of pastoral ministry into a ministry of itinerant preaching. In what country that was to be, was not yet clear to my wife Beverley and me. We suspected that it would be in the United States of America since for years I had had such a great desire to live there, a desire that I now know was placed in me by the Holy Spirit.

Loose Him and Let Him Go!

Some months before, while having my Quiet Time one morning, I was reading John chapter 11. As I read the words of Jesus' mighty act of raising Lazarus from the dead, I was profoundly impacted by an insight gleaned from the narrative:

> *"Now when He had said these things, He cried with a loud voice, 'Lazarus, come forth!'"*   (Verse 43)

When Jesus cried with a loud voice, *"Lazarus come forth,"* Lazarus did not come out of the tomb *"walking, and leaping and praising God"* like the lame man at the temple (Acts 3:8). Rather, he shuffled out of the tomb because of the grave clothes that were binding him and restricting his movements. Jesus had to instruct the bystanders to *"Loose him, and let him go"* (Verse 44). As I read those words, something began to stir deep within me. I knew that I was being commissioned by the Holy Spirit. He was giving me the direction for and a description of the ministry to which I knew He was calling me.

The deep irony of the situation was that I myself was in such bondage. The picture of Lazarus exiting the tomb unable to express the resurrection life because of the impediment of the grave-clothes, seemed to fit my own experience. More than that, it reflected what I observed in so many Christians around me. I knew without any doubt that I possessed resurrection life. Over time, though, I had come to the conviction, through observation of my own spiritual journey, that my grave-clothes were as great a hindrance to my expression of resurrection life as were the grave-clothes that bound Lazarus. I was so aware of the shackles of legalism, condemnation, anger, fear and so many other things that had crippled me and reduced me to a shuffle instead of a buoyant, joyous confidence as a son of the Father.

My heart began to rejoice as I realized that in the call to minister liberation to others, the Holy Spirit was giving me the inherent promise that liberty would come to me first. He was going to reveal to me how to get rid of my own bonds. That revelation would then equip me to remove the grave-clothes from others.

Receiving or Achieving – Faith or Obedience

Then came that Tuesday noon business-men's meeting where a lay pastor from a local Pentecostal church offended my theologically trained mind with the simple notion that receiving was the pathway to reigning. As he shared that message from Romans 5:17, the simplicity of his insight into the word began to collide rather explosively with my deeply entrenched belief system. In my mind, I found myself arguing my theological position that I had been taught and believed from childhood. More than that, I had taught the same principle to others while trying to live by it for all my years as a Christian. My sincere conviction was that obedience was the key word to a victorious Christian life.

I found an irrational anger rising in me as internally I reasoned the validity of my position. I became even more offended when he pointed with his finger (and every time he did so, it felt as though he was pointing at me) and asked: "Are you reigning?" I knew the answer deep inside. In spite of all my diligent discipline and hard work as the pastor of what I judged to be a healthy church, I was living in defeat.

Something, though, was beginning to change on the inside! I was about to undergo a profound paradigm shift that would totally change my life, my ministry and even my geographical location, as God would reveal to me the glorious truth that faith, rather than obedience, is the key to living a reigning life in this world.

At the time, I began to read Dr. D. Martyn Lloyd-Jones' commentary on Romans and in particular, the volume on "The Sons of God", comprised of sermons that he had preached from Romans 8 [D. Martyn Lloyd-Jones, *Romans – The Sons of God* (Grand Rapids, Michigan: Zondervan Publishing House, 1975)]. The further I read, the greater became the illumination. Realization dawned on my defeated but hungry heart that I was extremely ignorant of what it meant to be a son to the heavenly Father. Furthermore, I also realized how in my religious and family upbringing, I had, in my perception, been raised more as a servant than as a son.

So deep became the hunger to know the glorious freedom of being a son, that I resigned from the pastoral ministry at Gweru Baptist Church. Leaving Zimbabwe in December 1981, we moved with our children Tracy and Bradley back to South Africa to live with Bev's parents in East London. On January 2, I secluded myself in a travel-trailer at *Roebert's Holiday Resort* on the banks of the Igoda River, near East London. I was determined to fast, study and pray until I knew the reigning life that Paul was speaking of in Romans 5:17.

Passing On the Good News

The following chapters are the fruit of that month of January 1982, and the revelation that the precious Holy Spirit has imparted to me in subsequent years as I have lived in the sheer delight of being a son. It is my sincere prayer, that you, dear reader, will enter into the same liberty and enjoyment of being a son and daughter, as the grave clothes of servitude, legalism, rejection, performance and religion are stripped off you by the Holy Spirit through the truths contained in these pages. Some things that you will read, will possibly clash as violently with some of your cherished beliefs and religious traditions as they did with mine. I ask you not to allow the offense that might arise within your mind to block you reading all the way through the book. You might find your spirit saying "**Yes!**" to truths to which your mind is saying "No!" Allow the Holy Spirit, the Teacher, to bear witness to truth in your **spirit** even though your **mind** might be objecting because of the offense of the words you will read. My desire for you is that, just as I took the long journey home to the Father's house from the bondage of being a servant to the liberty of being a son, so the Spirit of Truth will bring you into that same glorious liberty.

"You shall know the truth, and the truth shall make you free."

John 8:32

CHAPTER 2

Once a Son...

"Jesus answered them, 'Most assuredly, I say to you, whoever commits sin is a slave of sin. And a slave does not abide in the house forever, but a son abides forever. Therefore if the Son makes you free, you shall be free indeed.'"   John 8:34-36

The Terror of Being Left Behind

None but those who have had a similar experience will understand the terror I experienced as a child when I would come home to an empty house. I would wonder if the "rapture" had taken place and I had been left behind. My father was a preacher of the gospel. The two major emphases of his ministry conspired to produce in my immature mind the terror that I often felt when entering our deserted family home.

His first emphasis in preaching was the imminent return of Jesus. Don't misunderstand me. There is nothing wrong with preaching the soon return of Jesus. It was just that in Dad's case, his focus was on a sudden and secret "rapture." He taught that Jesus was returning in a secret "rapture" to whisk

away those who are ready and leave those who are
not to go through the Great Tribulation. His many
sermons on Sunday and at mid-week meeting on
this sudden return and it's terrifying separation of
those who were ready and those who were not,
struck great fear into my young heart. The overwhelming burden of guilt and condemnation that I
carried made me certain that I was not ready. It was
this that caused me such anxiety when I returned
home to an empty house. For sure, Jesus had
returned and had caught my family away. I was the
only one who had been left behind!

The second emphasis of Daddy's preaching that
so affected me concerned the fear of 'losing' my
salvation. Coming as he did from a denominational
and theological background that contested any man's
right to believe that his salvation was absolutely secure, there were many times that Daddy preached
with stern conviction the warning of Hebrews 12:14:
"Holiness, without which no one will see the Lord."
Because I did not feel that I was holy, I never felt
ready to see God. Assurance of salvation remained
elusive to me. I was so sincere in my desire to
know that I was a child of God, but it seemed that I
could never attain to that knowledge.

I often responded to invitations that my Daddy
gave in the evangelistic services that we had each
Sunday night. Each time, I would walk the aisle to
the front to receive Jesus 'again' as savior. And

yet, although I was as serious as I could possibly be, I could never come to a place of peace and assurance that I was really accepted by God, that my sins were truly forgiven and that should Jesus return, I would be ready to *"see the Lord."*

You are Not Acting Like a Christian

This hopelessness was reinforced by my father's regular observation that I was not "behaving like a Christian." If my assurance of salvation was based on my acting like a Christian, which I interpreted as living an exemplary life of holiness, then what hope did I have of being saved and therefore seeing the Lord? Obviously, I reasoned in my young mind, I could not possibly be saved if I was not acting like a true Christian should. I could not distinguish between the fruit of salvation and the basis of salvation. Hence I lived in perpetual fear, guilt and condemnation.

The Son's Liberation Produces Free Sons

What a stark contrast to the affirming and comforting words of Jesus in John 8! Listen to what Jesus declared as the state of one who has experienced His liberating power: *"And a slave does not abide in the house forever, but a son abides forever. Therefore if the Son makes you free, you shall be free indeed,"* (John 8:35-36).

The occasion upon which Jesus spoke these words was a follow-up to many believing in Him. He was showing them the difference between their relationship to God under the Old Covenant and under the New.

Under the Old Covenant, they were under the restriction of law through which every transgression, being clearly defined, is also severely judged. Since *"by the law is the knowledge of sin"* (Romans 3:20), everyone living under that law was summarily judged as a transgressor and became painfully aware of two things: their inability to keep that law due to their enslavement to sin, and the resulting sense of condemnation, guilt and frustration. Jesus reinforced the hopelessness of the situation when He declared in John 8:34: *"Whoever commits sin is a slave of sin."*

In contrast to this utterly hopeless position of slavery, Jesus announced His mission. He had come to liberate us into a liberty as real as His own as the Son of God: *"Therefore if the Son makes you free, you shall be free indeed"* (John 8:36).

The Tenuous Position of A Servant

Jesus then followed up the declaration of sin's slavery in verse 34 with a comparison of a servant and a son: *"A servant abideth not in the house forever: But the son abideth ever,"* (Verse 35, KJV).

A servant, by very definition of the name, is there to serve. His (or her) relationship to his master (or mistress) is performance based. His daily responsibility consists of entering his master's house, receiving his assignments, and setting about fulfilling them to the best of his ability. Should he fulfill them to his master's pleasure, he is then appropriately rewarded. He can then retire to the servant's quarters being assured of his master's pleasure, the satisfaction of his wage, and the assurance that the relationship is secure. Should he fail to do his master's will, some or all of the following may happen:

1. The anger of his displeased master may be vented upon him.
2. The wages promised as a reward could be withheld as a punishment.
3. Some other form of punishment could also be meted to him (In the case of a slave this might also include a physical beating).
4. His employment could be terminated.

When Your Best is Not Good Enough

Jesus added to the frustrating hopelessness of relationship to God as a servant by His declaration in Luke 17:10. Speaking before the establishing of the new covenant and the coming of the Holy Spirit, the Spirit of adoption, He said:

"So likewise you, when you have done all those things which you are commanded, say, 'We are unprofita-ble servants. We have done what was our duty to do.'"

If you see yourself as a servant and believe that your acceptance and approval by God is based on your performance as a servant, be prepared for great frustration. Though you might perform all that you believe God has commanded you to do, you will never escape from the damning sense that you should have done more. Well-intentioned preachers thundering from the pulpit will exacerbate the problem by heaping condemnation on you as they remind you of the "sins of omission" besides the "sins of commission." You are guilty before God, they declare, for what you failed to do as much as for the transgressions that you did commit.

The most that a servant can hope for is not very much. At the end of the day, if he has done the master's will, he receives a commendation from his master with its accompanying financial remuneration. If he has failed to please, he will be berated for failure to measure up. The servant then leaves the master's house and the intimacy of the evening family relationships and goes to his quarters. As he lies down, all he has to look forward to is another day of **performance** in an attempt to please his master and, hopefully, earn a reward. *"A slave does*

not abide in the house forever. " There are no eve-
nings of intimate family interaction. There is no
assurance that tomorrow will not be his last day of
secure employment.

The Permanency of Sonship

In contrast to the tenuous, temporary (because it is
performance based) nature of the servant/master
relationship, Jesus declares that a son *"abides forever, "* (verse 35). What makes the difference? In
contrast to the servant, the son's relationship to and
acceptance by the father is not performance based,
but is based on a birth. The son **will** do the father's
will, but that flows out of the relationship and is not
a condition to the relationship. Because he loves
and respects his father, a son will serve his father
faithfully and diligently. In fact, a son, in contrast
to a servant who might be a 'clock-watcher' and try
to get by with doing the least possible, will often go
beyond what is expected of him simply because he
is a son and loves his father. At times, the father
might be disappointed and displeased with his son's
behavior but, nevertheless, he remains the father
and the son remains the son irrespective of his
performance.

Once a son...**always a son!**

CHAPTER 3

Hearing the Father's Heart

"With fervent desire I have desired to eat this Passover with you before I suffer; for I say to you, I will no longer eat of it until it is fulfilled in the kingdom of God."　　　　Luke 22:15-16

The force of Jesus words is breathtaking! Our English translations do not do justice to the intensity of the words Jesus used. The Greek word used twice is *epithumia* which is, more usually, translated *"lust."* Jesus literally says, *"With lust have I lusted to eat this Passover."* His double use of the word expresses a great fervency of desire. What is it about this Passover meal that caused Jesus to express Himself with such intensity?

The answer lies in His use of the word *"fulfilled."* He was about to fulfill all of the type and shadow of the Passover meal with its sacrificial lamb. Because it was to be fulfilled in His death on the cross the next day, this would also be the occasion for the instituting of a replacement meal. The New Covenant meal would confirm and celebrate a new relationship for man with God just as the original Passover meal had been the celebration of God's redemption of His people out of Egypt to bring them into relationship with Himself.

The Inter-covenantal Transition in the Lord's Supper

We have generally overlooked the inter-covenantal dividing line drawn by this meal in separating the old from the new. We recognize the significance of Jesus death, burial and resurrection as a watershed in revelation of the fulfillment of the old and the ushering in of the new. However, we often overlook the powerful contrasts that He drew between the old and new on the occasion of this meal. We fail to recognize that the Passover meal, representing the Old Covenant, was being superseded by a new meal announcing a New Covenant.

A new covenant means the whole basis for relating to God was changing. Jesus, in his post-meal discourse, announced the many changes that were being initiated through the meal and what it portrayed. Prayer, for example, was moved into a new dimension of asking in Jesus' name (John 16:24) and being absolutely assured that God the Father will give us whatever we ask in that name!

The transition announced by Jesus that relates to this study is found in John 15:15:

*"No longer do I call you servants, for a servant does not know what his master is doing; but I have called you **friends**, for all things that I heard from My Father I have made known to you."*

The word *"friends"* that Jesus uses here is a covenant word. Abraham was called God's friend because
of God's covenant with him. Jesus was identifying
a dramatic change in relationships that was occur-
ring in that moment.

The Ignorance of a Servant

No master takes his servant into his confidence and
shares the deep secrets of his heart with him. Such
familiarity would breed contempt and destroy the
formality necessary to maintain authority. Note
Solomon's warning in Proverbs 29:21 against raising a servant in familiarity: *"He who pampers his
servant from childhood will have him as a son in the
end."*

Jesus' implication in John 15:15 is that the master
only communicates to his servant the information
he needs to fulfill his responsibility and no more.
That communication consists primarily of commandments for the servant to obey. The master is
not obligated to tell the servant "why" he should do
what the master desires. The servant does not know
what his master is doing, i.e. his motivation and
purpose, but knows what he is to do.

It is so tragic that so many Christians live at that
level. Because they see themselves as servants rather
than sons, their communication with God is limited
to finding out what God wants them to do. They

never feel comfortable claiming the promises of God without underlining the commandments of God. They do not expect God to reveal the deep secrets of His heart to them. They are always looking for someone to "get a word from God" for them or to pray for them because they fear that their own prayers are not heard.

The Bread of His Presence

Such thinking reveals a lamentable misunderstanding of the covenant meal. The Old Testament antecedent for the bread in the New Testament meal is the *"showbread"* (Exodus 25:30) or, literally, the *"bread of His face,"* or the *"bread of His presence."* Remember how, in 1 Samuel 21:6, Ahimelech gave David and his men the only bread available, the showbread, *"which had been taken from before the Lord."* The showbread represented unrestricted, uninterrupted, face to face communion with God.

When the elders of Israel ascended Mount Sinai with Moses and Aaron, *"they saw God and they ate and they drank,"* (Exodus 24:10). Just as Jesus was revealed to the two Emmaus Road travelers in the breaking of the bread, so the bread of the new covenant meal guarantees to the believer the unveiling of the face of God. He wants to be intimate with us and can be so, since we are no longer servants. Jesus than declared us to be on a par with

Himself as far as revelation from the Father is concerned: *"**All things** that I heard...I have made know to you,"* (John 15:15).

At the same time, He was introducing them to His successor, the Holy Spirit whom He called *"the Spirit of Truth"* (John 14:17) who would teach them all things (14:26) and guide them into all truth (16:13). *"He will take of what is Mine and declare it to you,"* Jesus stated (John 16:14). He then interpreted what His use of the word *"Mine"* entails:

*All things that the Father has are **Mine**.*

John 16:15

The Spirit of Revelation

I will never forget the day in 1981, while reading in 1 Corinthians 1 and 2 in my daily devotional time, when the truth suddenly blazed in my soul that the Holy Spirit had come to me to reveal to me the *"deep things of God,"* (2:10). For so long I had lived in verse 9: *"Eye has not seen...!"* Knowing God's will was more a matter of **hindsight** than **foresight**.

But now the Holy Spirit was opening my spiritual eyes to the revelation that *"God **has** revealed them to us through His Spirit,"* (2:10).

The Spirit of the World

What had been the blockage? Paul called it *'the spirit of the world'* (2:12). Receiving the spirit of the world will prevent me from receiving revelation of all the things freely given to me by God. From the context of these two chapters in 1 Corinthians, we learn that the spirit of the world boasts in human wisdom and exalts human reason above the revelation of God. In a subtle way, through my five years of theological education I had slowly imbibed and succumbed to a worldly spirit that exalted human reason. I had to come face to face with the realization that some of my teachers, authors of books and historical theological figures, held more authority in my thinking than the simple truth of the Word of God. Like Peter on the mount of transfiguration, I wanted to set other great prophetic figures on the same level of importance and authority as Jesus, who is the Word! It was the teaching of great but finite men of God whose words had brought pollution to the pure stream of revelation that was my birthright as a son of God.

Why did I feel so distant from God and so sure that He was extremely reluctant to speak to me? The answer came as He began to reveal to me my position as a son! Just as the spirit of the world and the Spirit of revelation are mutually exclusive, so a spirit of servitude will exclude me from receiving the

Spirit of sonship and leave me feeling like a servant or a conditionally-loved and rejected stepchild.

I had been infected by both spirits that are closely linked to each other. The spirit of the world had produced in me a spirit of bondage. The traditions of men had ensnared me in a religious performance that Jesus had come to do away with. Men's wisdom had kept me in bondage under a heavy yoke of striving to be acceptable to God. I was beginning to see the traps that had ensnared me through the fear of man. I had reverenced man's word over the liberating truth of God's word.

I was also beginning to see what a glorious dimension of relationship Jesus has ushered us into. In contrast to my erroneous conceptions of the reluctance of God to speak to me, I began to see the Father's desire for me to know the **deep** things of His heart. He does not want me, as a son, to know Him and judge Him by his external actions but rather to know His heart and therefore to understand His ways!

No Longer Do I Call You Servants

One of the great misconceptions prevalent amongst Christians is that Jesus' teaching of the servant/ master relationship in His parables is applicable to our living today. Because of a lack of understanding of the purpose of His teaching during His earthly ministry and the transition marked by the institution of this covenant meal, people live under a burden of performance that was terminated through the cross.

What was Jesus' purpose in teaching so extensively on the requirements of the law? He had come, He said, to uphold the law in order to ultimately fulfill it. In the light of this, He was inflexible in teaching the stringent requirements of the law. This was preparatory to His glorious work of nailing the *"hand-writing of requirements that was against us"* to the cross (Colossians 2:14). Having instituted the covenant meal, and introduced His disciples to the *"new covenant in My blood,"* (Luke 22:20), Jesus then declared the transition in their relationship from servant/master to one of covenant friendship. As friends, they were now in a position to possess as their very own whatever He had received from the Father.

New Covenant, New Relationship

The subject of covenant cannot be fully expounded in this book. Suffice it to say that the New Covenant is not between God on the one hand and us on the other. If that were the case, the promises and blessings of the covenant would be dependent upon our fully satisfying all of God's righteous requirements to be accepted before Him. They would no

longer be by promise through faith but would be a
reward for the obedient works of the law. The glorious wonder of the New Covenant is that God cut covenant with Himself. He became man in His Son,
Jesus Christ. Then, as man, He fully satisfied His
own demands for righteousness, shed His blood as a
sacrifice for man's failure to live in obedience to
those righteous demands, and by that same blood cut
covenant with Himself on man's behalf. The perfect
God-man could perfectly represent God to man and
man to God. Only by Him being fully God and fully
man could we be assured of the perfection and ac-
ceptability of what He did on our behalf.

Now, through the new birth, I am united with
Christ in that sacrificial death and am raised with
Him to enter into the enjoyment of uninterrupted
communion with God the Father and participation
in the Son's inheritance of **all** that belonged to the
Father. In Christ I am in covenant with God. In
Christ, I become a son and therefore an heir, not a
servant who works for a wage.

Paul gave us a magnificent insight into God's purpose for His children in Ephesians 1:3-5:

*"Blessed be the God and Father of our Lord Jesus
Christ, who has blessed us with every spiritual
blessing in the heavenly places in Christ...having
predestined us to adoption as sons by Jesus Christ to
Himself, according to the good pleasure of His will."*

God has not predestined us to an assignment as servants with the nebulous hope of a wage, but to *"adoption as sons,"* and with that adoption, comes the inheritance of *"every spiritual blessing."* Note that Paul said that God has already blessed us. The inheritance is already ours.

So many Christians have never entered into the full enjoyment and appropriation of their inheritance. What is keeping them from it? How can we be free from this oppressive frustration of feeling like an outsider looking in? How do we escape from feeling second-class, stepchildren or servants.

Into experiencing the joy of **belonging** in the Father's house? How do we move from the ignorance of a servant to the shared intimacy of Jesus' revelation of the Father through the Holy Spirit? How do I come to the place of hearing the Father's heart and knowing the deep things of God?

The answer to these questions lies in the glorious gift and ministry of the Holy Spirit. We are about to explore the uniqueness of His role under the new covenant in bringing us into the enjoyment of our birthright, which is intimacy and inheritance as sons and daughters of God.

CHAPTER 4

The Spirit of Sonship

"For you did not receive the spirit of bondage again to fear, but you received the Spirit of adoption by Whom we cry out, 'Abba, Father.' The Spirit Himself bears witness with our spirit that we are the children of God, and if children, then heirs – heirs of God and joint heirs with Christ."

Romans 8:15-17

"Again!" As I studied Romans 8 back in the travel-trailer at Igoda River mouth back in January 1982, it was that word *"again"* that impacted me so powerfully. Through reading D. Martyn Lloyd-Jones book *Romans – The Sons of God*, referred to in chapter one, a fire had been lit in my spirit that could not be quenched until I knew the truth. Why did I continually live in such performance, condemnation and frustration?

Lloya-Jones' book was the only book, besides my Bible, that I felt the Holy Spirit wanted me to take out to Igoda as I embarked on my quest. I spent many hours studying verse 15, checking the original Greek language, translating, meditating and praying over each word.

Though some of the conclusions that I came to differed from those arrived at in the book, nevertheless the truths and insights of Dr. Lloyd-Jones were being used by God to precipitate a radical transformation in my entire theological foundation.

The Spirit of Bondage

"For you did not receive the spirit of bondage again to fear, but you received the Spirit of adoption by whom we cry out, 'Abba, Father.'"   Romans 8:15

The first mind-blowing truth that impacted me was that here was another mutually exclusive verse such as had begun to change my thinking the previous year. Just as the *"spirit of the world"* excludes my receiving the *"Spirit of revelation,"* in the same way, receiving *"the spirit of bondage"* excludes my receiving, at the same time, *"the Spirit of adoption."* What is more, Paul calls it a *"spirit."* We are not then dealing simply with ignorance of truth or an emotional state, but are dealing with a spiritual problem produced by ignorance at best and by deception at worst. We are confronted here by a demonic activity of our archenemy, Satan, to keep us from enjoying the position that Jesus has brought us into through His glorious work at the cross.

The Law of Sin and Death

In the second verse of the chapter, Paul had already declared the glorious liberating power of the Holy Spirit imparting to me life in Christ Jesus. That life has liberated me from the *"law of sin and death."* Paul explained in Chapter Seven just how that law operates. By the law of sin and death, I become aware that I am a sinner; if there were no law, I would have no consciousness of sin (see Romans 7:7-8). The moment I become awakened to the fact that there is a law against things that I am doing, sin becomes present reality and the death sentence is passed on me (verse 9).

The law of the Spirit of life in Christ Jesus

When I come into Christ, the new law of the Spirit does not condemn me for my failure to measure up. *"There is no condemnation,"* Romans 8:1 declares. Instead it points me to the *"life in Christ Jesus,"* the Anointed One (Verse 2). *Christos* is the Greek word translated or, rather, transliterated "Christ". It means "the Anointed One" and should be translated as such. My new life as a believer is in the Anointed One, Jesus. By that wonderful anointing that is upon Him, the Holy Spirit imparts life to me in place of the death that comes on me through the Mosaic law. He will never minister law and condemnation to me because that **always** produces death: *"The letter* *kills...the ministry of death...the ministry of condemnation, "* (2 Corinthians 3:7, 9).

The purpose of the Spirit, however, is to minister life! Paul says, *"The letter kills, but the Spirit gives life, "* (2 Corinthians 3:6). He cannot therefore ever minister the law to a believer. In fact, nowhere does the Bible teach us that He convicts us of sin. That is His work in the world: *"And when He has come, He will convict **the world** of sin, and of righteousness, and of judgement, "* (*John 16:8*).

The word for *"convict"* means "mental convincing." We have already seen that the Holy Spirit's purpose in us believers is spiritual revelation, not mental convincing. Mental persuasion is the work of *"the spirit of the world"* that we studied in the last chapter. In John 16:13, Jesus reveals his ministry to us, His disciples: *"He will guide you into all truth. "* His ministry to the believer is to reveal the fullness of life in the Anointed One, Jesus. That revelation then exposes sin and death in the believer's life. He then guides us out of the deception of sin into the liberty of truth and the reality of life in Christ Jesus.

Receiving the Spirit of Bondage Again

However, anyone who has been a Christian for any time at all will have discovered that there are many others who desire to put you back under law. Some do this intentionally as did the false teachers in Galatia who utilized the manipulation, intimidation and control of what Paul calls witchcraft, (Galatians 3:1). Some, on the other hand, do this totally unintentionally. In all probability, the person who prayed with you when you received Jesus as Savior, in an effort to conserve the fruit just picked, advised you in words such as these: "Now that you are a Christian, you need to read the Bible, pray daily, attend Church, witness and give." That is not bad advice because those are ways in which your new life would be expressed and conserved. The problem is this: We have an enemy! Deception, distortion and confusion are his chief weapons. He soon turns what was given to you as and exhortation into a commandment to beat you mercilessly with condemnation and guilt! "You need to" becomes "you must!"

What that does to me is bring me into bondage *"again."* I receive a *"spirit of bondage"* the moment I revert to trying to please God and be accepted through what I do. That, in effect, is the essence of religion. Religion is, by definition, man's systems of behavior and rituals of worship by which man seeks to be made acceptable to his god. The law and its demands for obedience were done away with as a basis of relationship to God in Jesus' death on the cross. To adhere to the law, as a basis of acceptance with God, now becomes bondage to *"the command-*

ments and doctrines of men" and *"self-imposed religion,"* (Colossians 2:22-23). Righteousness is no longer a reward for keeping the law perfectly but now is a gift received by simple faith. Remember the verse that started my journey! *"Much more those who receive...the gift of righteousness,"* (Romans 5:17).

What's more, those helpful words of advice turned by the *"accuser of our brethren,"* (Revelation 12:10) into a commandment, lead to a fear motivation in what I do as a Christian. Paul said, *"You did not receive the spirit of bondage again to fear."* We can correctly translate it *"leading to fear."* What fear was Paul talking about? To understand that let us study what John taught about fear and love.

Perfect Love Casts Out All Fear

"There is no fear in love; but perfect love casts out fear, because fear involves torment. But he who fears has not been made perfect in love."

1 John 4:18

John said that *"there is no fear in love."* In fact, the presence of fear shows an immaturity in knowing and receiving God's love. Why is that? *"Because,"* he said, *"fear involves torment,"* or, more accurately, fear has to do with punishment. The only one who fears is one who does not understand the perfect work of Jesus in paying, not only the price of redemption for us, but also paying the penalty of our sin. That means that since He took the punishment for our sin, we need have no fear of punishment. We certainly will be disciplined by our heavenly Father, but that discipline is not punitive but wholly redemptive, *"that we may be partakers of His holiness,"* (Hebrews 12:10). His discipline is therefore not retroactive (looking back in anger and vengeance at what we have done), but anticipatory, expecting that His loving correction as a Father will produce transformation into His likeness.

Perfect love casts out all fear. The presence of fear indicates the absence of perfect love. Therefore, if I have fear, **any fear** (John did not qualify that word), that is the surest sign that I do not understand my position as a son and am still in bondage to performance: trying to please God and be acceptable through obedience to commandments. Fear enters when I feel that I am not reaching the acceptable standard of performance and might be rejected by God. In contrast, the son is so secure in his Father's love, that he is able to rest in the promises that His Father has made of protection, provision and His abiding presence.

Respect and Honor Vs. Dread and Terror

"But," someone may ask, "isn't the fear of the Lord a healthy thing? Doesn't Solomon say: *'The fear of the Lord is the beginning of wisdom'* (Proverbs 9:10)?" That is a different fear entirely. That is a reverential fear that honors and regards highly an esteemed person who is worthy of that honor. The fear that we are dealing with is a fear based on a performance standard of relationship that dreads the consequences of not measuring up to a real or imagined standard of acceptance.

Let me use a personal illustration which, though imperfect, might help us to understand the difference. Because of the unconditional nature of the love relationship that my wife, Bev, and I enjoy, I do not fear her rejection should I make a mistake. I know that she loves me in spite of the dumb things that I might do. However, because I regard her and esteem her so highly, there is a strong motivation within me not to do anything that would cause her grief nor that would threaten the beauty and intimacy of the relationship that we enjoy. I do not fear the break up of our marriage should I make a mistake. Through twenty-five years of marriage we have proven our unconditional love for, and our commitment to, each other and to the permanence of our marriage. We do not walk on eggshells around each other fearing that should one partner make a mistake, the other would pack up and leave. Love and the trust foundation of our marriage has cast out that fear! What I do fear is doing anything that might grieve her and wound her spirit.

In a similar yet far greater way, the revelation of the Father's commitment to me in the new covenant removes all fear of rejection. Why? Because He has made me a son! Remember Jesus said, *"The Son abides forever,"* (John 8:35). The security of my position as a son cradled in the perfect, unconditional love of the Father's embrace drives out every anxious thought of the Father not finding me pleasing and acceptable. I need not fear anything that comes my way knowing that my Father loves me and is committed to my protection and to provide for every need.

However, because of His unfailing love and goodness to me, my deep desire as a son is to do nothing that would displease Him and grieve His Holy Spirit. Out of that reverential fear I gladly obey Him, not because my acceptance is dependent upon that obedience, but because His great love for me motivates me to do what pleases Him.

The Basis of Our Acceptance

We have already seen that Jesus taught that living as a servant always leaves us with a sense of incompleteness, a fear that we have not done enough. The law is an onerous and merciless slave driver. It is never satisfied, placated or pleased. Our best falls far short of the perfection it demands. If we revert to trying to be pleasing to God through obedience to the demands of the law, the fear of not being good enough will be the result. We will *"again"* receive that *"spirit of bondage"*.

In contrast to that, Paul affirmed the positive truth of what happens when I become a child of God:

"But you received the Spirit of adoption by whom we cry out, 'Abba, Father!'   Romans 8:15

1. *"Abba"* is the Aramaic word that is equivalent to our modern day 'Daddy.' It implies familiarity and intimacy.

2. *"Adoption"* is the English translation of a Greek word that literally translated means "the placing as a son." The position in which I am placed by the Holy Spirit is much more that a mere legal adoption. The new birth is the operative power by which that placement takes place. I receive the Father's nature and Spirit. It is His Spirit, under the New Covenant, who uniquely imparts a covenantal authority and power to **become** a son of God. As a son, I now possess the full rights of sonship, including inheritance!

3. *"We cry out."* The spirit within us, awakened by the moving upon it of the grace of God revealed in the gospel, is stirred to cry out by faith in the truth, "Daddy, Papa, Abba, Father!" In Galatians 4:6 (we will study this passage in more depth in the next chapter) Paul said that the Spirit cries

out. We cry, He cries! I believe that is what Paul is implying in Romans 8:16: *"The Spirit Himself bears witness with our spirit that we are children of God."* The word Paul used translated *"with"* means "alongside," as in a duet. When I, in simple faith begin to cry out in confession that God is now my Daddy, His Holy Spirit comes alongside my spirit and echoes into the deep recesses of my spirit His cry, "Daddy! Abba! Father!"

4. *"The Spirit of His Son"* (Galatians 4:6). What a glorious truth! The Spirit of sonship whom God now sends to indwell me, is the same Spirit of sonship who dwelled in Jesus! Why would we ever fear rejection by God our Father when the Spirit within us is the same Spirit Who lived in Jesus? Why would we ever think that we need rules and commandments to regulate our lives when the Spirit indwelling us is the same Spirit of sonship Who caused Jesus to perfectly please the Father? Our reverting to living by rules and performance is an insult to the grace and goodness of our Father who has sent **the same Spirit of sonship,** who motivated Jesus' life of obedience to the Father, to live in us!

5. *"Cry."* No timidity and tentativeness here! This is strong crying based on strong conviction! You might start a little timidly and feel embarrassed at the thought of calling God 'Daddy!' But as you

begin, and you hear the echo of His Spirit in your heart as you speak, you soon gain confidence, momentum and volume until you are **crying out**! Never fear extreme emotions in the Father's presence. It is only the man-made religious system that will tell you not to be emotional! Remember, Jesus prayed with *"vehement cries and tears"* and was heard, (Hebrews 5:7). Shout it loud, shout it long!, **"DADDY, ABBA, FATHER!"**

What You Say Is What You Get

It is abundantly clear from the Scriptures that we live in the fruit of what we have spoken with our mouths (Proverbs 12:14, 13:2, 18:20-21). Salvation is yours because, by faith in the gospel, you confessed: *"Jesus is Lord!"* (Romans 10:9-10). In the same way, the assurance of your position as a son (or daughter) through the echoing witness of the Holy Spirit, must begin with your confession of faith in the revelation of God's covenant. If you keep on confessing yourself as a servant (and an unprofitable one at that), you will never break through into the wonderful joy and liberty that comes with the knowledge of being God's son and daughter. Your confession must come into agreement with what God says.

Some years ago, I was involved with one of the board members of our ministry, Bill James, in taking men up into the mountains of Colorado on a hunting/fellowship/eating trip, with a great deal of emphasis on the latter! Bill has organized these trips for many years. On two occasions, one near Black Mountain in the Gunnison National Forest near Maher and one in the Danforth Hills near Meaker, I taught the men these truths concerning sonship. There is a precious exercise in faith that God has used so many times to break people through into assurance. After teaching them on the importance of the confession of our lips in this whole matter of assurance of sonship, I encouraged them to climb up one of the surrounding hills to a point where they felt comfortable enough that no one would hear them.

Then, beginning perhaps in a soft voice, they were to begin to confess the truth of the Word, even though emotionally they might not feel it. Sometimes they would need to stand against a ferocious counter-attack of the accusations of the enemy. He did not want the truth to come from their lips! However, when they would begin to say, "Abba" or "Daddy" or "Papa God," they would discover something supernatural beginning to take place. They would begin to hear the echo of the Holy Spirit as he came alongside them and replied to their confession of faith, "Abba, Father." The louder their confession became, the louder would come His responding affirmation. They cried...He cried!

Many of them would return from the mountains with a radiant joy in their hearts and on their faces.

Find a Shouting Place

It is very likely that many of you who read this book are under a burden of rejection, performance and hopelessness because you feel that you can never break through into an assurance of your sonship. Here is God's solution. It is by faith! If you are waiting for God to come to you personally and give you a subjective assurance, you may have a long wait. He has already come to you in the person of His son. Now the initiative is yours! Find a place where you will not be disturbed or cause a disturbance! By faith, begin to cry out what the Word declares is the truth. You are a son or a daughter. He is your Father. You have a God-given right to come boldly into His presence and cry out!

Firstly, repent of the words of your mouth that have contradicted the revelation of the purpose of Jesus' work on the cross. He did not come to redeem servants. He came to bring *"sons to glory,"* (Hebrews 2:10). You are not a servant! You are a son! You are a daughter!

Now, begin to cry out, **"Abba!" "Father!"**

CHAPTER 5

No Longer a Servant

"Now I say that the heir, as long as he is a child, does not differ at all from a slave, though he is master of all, but is under guardians and stewards until the time appointed by the father. Even so we, when we were children, were in bondage under the elements of the world. But when the fullness of time had come, God sent forth His Son, born of a woman, born under the law, to redeem those who were under the law, that we might receive the adoption as sons. And because you are sons, God has sent forth the Spirit of His Son into your hearts, crying out, 'Abba, Father!' Therefore you are no longer a slave but a son, and if a son, then an heir of God through Christ." Galatians 4:1-7

"You are saved to serve!" That has been a watchword for many generations of Christians. For countless millions of believers, for most of the past two thousand years, there has been no higher purpose for their salvation than to 'serve' the Lord while in this life. As with many lies that bring men into captivity, there is truth in that statement. However, for many, that statement has damned them to a life of performance, condemnation and guilt.

Our Restored Position

God's purpose in saving you was not to make you a servant but, as we have already seen, to *"adoption,"* which, we discovered, means *"to place as a son,"* (Romans 8:15). He has predestined you to *"adoption as sons,"* (Ephesians 1:5). The intent of His Father's heart is to, ultimately, bring *"many sons to glory,"* (Hebrews 2:10). The clearest statement of His purpose in the New Covenant in this regard is recorded in Galatians 4:1-7, the passage that heads this chapter.

Having shown us that the law kept us as slaves, Paul declared:

"But when the fullness of the time had come, God sent forth His Son, born of a woman, born under the law, to redeem those who were under the law, that we might receive the adoption as sons,"

(Verses 4 and 5).

Jesus had to be *"born of a woman"* in order to be a perfect high priest on man's behalf. He had to be born under the law in order that, by his perfect obedience, He might fulfill the demands of that law upon the descendants of Adam. Only then could we be brought out from the bondage of being under a schoolmaster or overseer. Paul said that that condition pertained *"Until the time appointed by the*

father," (Verse 2). An immature child, though he is
the heir to all the father's wealth, is no better than a
slave, *"though he is master of all,"* (Verse 1).

God's Creative Purpose

God created man to have dominion over all of the
works of His hands, having placed him just beneath
Himself. David, under the inspiration of the Holy
Spirit, ascribed a high place of glory and honor to
us:

> *"What is man that You are mindful of him,*
> *And the son of man that You visit him?*
> *For You made him a little lower than the angels,*
> *And You have crowned him with glory and honor.*
> *You have made him to have dominion over the works*
> *of Your hands;*
> *You have put all things under his feet."*
>
> Psalm 8:4-6

There is a tragic mistranslation of the Hebrew
original in this passage. The Hebrew word translated *"angels"* is the word *"Elohim"* which should
be translated *"God."* We are not lower than the
angels are. We were created to be sons, to have
dominion over the works of His hands with all things
under our feet, (Verse 6). The angels, in fact, are
"ministering spirits sent forth to minister for (on

behalf of) *those who will inherit salvation,"* (Hebrews 1:14). God, having created man in His own image, assigned him a dominant place in all of His creation. However, man's fall into rebellion and sin cost him that honored place as man conceded the dominion to the usurper, Satan.

But now, in the fullness of time, the Son had come to redeem sons from under the curse of the law. The law had been given to reveal the sin of Adam's race and to pass God's judgment on it. His purpose for us in redemption is **restoration**, not to some position of subservience, but to a position of sonship.

If A Son, Then An Heir

In the restoration to sonship comes a restoration to dominion and being *"master of all,"* (Galatians 4:1). This comes to us, not by our inherent goodness, but by His adoption of us. In fact, Jesus, our covenant Head, has inherited all things. Now through faith in Him as our covenant Representative, we become joint heirs with Him. *"Therefore you are no longer a slave but a son, and if a son, then an heir of God through Christ,"* (Galatians 4:7). We become:

*Heirs of God **and joint heirs with Christ.***
                                        Romans 8:17

Hallelujah! What a glorious salvation! No wonder

Satan wants us to continue thinking of ourselves merely as servants. If we ever rise up in faith in the revelation of our position as heirs, we will start to take back what is rightfully ours, exercise the dominion that God has given to us, and plunder the enemy who has stolen what belongs to us.

The Fundamental Difference Between Sons and Servants

It is absolutely vital that we catch the significance of what Paul is declaring here. Remember that we saw that angels are sent to minister on behalf of heirs (Hebrews 1:17). There are so many promises in the New Testament made to heirs and so much that is classified as an inheritance. If we do not grasp the significance of inheritance, we will have missed the entire good news of the gospel.

A servant serves his master hoping for a reward. A son does not earn his inheritance. It is a **gift**. It is not because of his worthiness or deserving nature that the inheritance comes to him. Rather it devolves upon him because of his birth. He is born a son and therefore an heir. In the case of legal adoption as practiced in Paul's time, it was impossible for an adoptive father to disinherit his son. The adoptive son's rights are more legally secure than a natural-born son.

The Servant and Self-Evaluation

So many Christians still see themselves in a position of having to earn the blessings of the Father. By constant self-examination, they are betraying their servant mentality that allows them to feel deserving of the rewarded blessings only if they are satisfied with their performance. The constant need to do more and the accompanying frustration of never feeling that they have done enough mark their lives.

If that is where you are, dear reader, let me exhort you to begin to open yourself to the Holy Spirit in a new way. He is *"the Spirit of adoption."* He is the same Spirit of sonship who indwelt Jesus as a son. Paul tells us that *"God has sent forth the Spirit of His Son into your hearts, crying out, 'Abba, Father,'" (Galatians 4:6).* The same Spirit of sonship who assured Jesus of His Father's acceptance and love and motivated His life of obedience to the Father has been sent forth to bring you the same assurance and inspire the same obedience.

In Summary

Before we move on, it will help us immensely to summarize what we have learnt so far in discovering what the Bible teaches us concerning the difference between a servant and a son.

1. A servant does not abide in the house forever

because his relationship to the master is task oriented. The son's relationship is permanent based on a birth and is not dependent on performance.

2. A master does not take a servant into his confidence and reveal the intimacies of his heart. A covenant son is brought into a place of "friendship," of intimate communion and revelation of heart matters.

3. The servant's relationship with his master is governed by fear:
   a. The fear of not measuring up to the master's expectations
   b. The fear of not receiving the reward for his services
   c. The fear of punishment should he fail to do the master's will
   d. The fear that, should he not fully please the master, his services could be terminated

   In contrast to the servant, the son lives in the security of perfect love, which casts out all fear.

4. The servant works so as to earn a reward. A son, being an heir, possesses the Father's wealth without earning or deserving it.

As we proceed into the following chapters, you will be able to identify more easily what Spirit you are receiving: The *"spirit of bondage"* and servitude, or *"the Spirit of adoption,"* the Spirit of sonship.

CHAPTER 6

Coming Home To the Father's House

"Then all the tax collectors and the sinners drew near to Him to hear Him. And the Pharisees and scribes complained, saying, 'This man receives sinners and eats with them.'" Luke 15:1-2

Jesus' Scandalous Behavior

God...receives...sinners! In the religious minds of the Pharisees and scribes, these three words could never be used together. This was the principal reason that they were convinced that Jesus was a blaspheming impostor. If He really was from God, as He claimed, then He would know what kind of people were pressing around Him and would most certainly reject them. To **receive** them was utterly unthinkable. Worse than that, Jesus had the gall to allow these sinners to even touch Him! He surely could not be from God for, if He were, He would understand the contaminating effects on personal holiness of allowing contact with unclean things.

What irrevocably convinced them that Jesus was a fraud, was His audacity to not only receive sinners, but, scandalously, to **eat** with them! In their minds, this was the ultimate negation of divine sanction or origin. Jesus simply could not be from God! When they observed all the tax-collectors and sinners (those who did not attend the synagogue and practice the ritual of Judaism) coming to Jesus to listen to Him teach, they complained: *"This man receives sinners and eats with them."*

The Misnamed Parables

In response to their criticism, Jesus tells the Pharisees and scribes three parables, which we identify as the parables of The Lost Sheep, The Lost Coin and The Prodigal Son. Unfortunately, in so naming them, we have deflected attention away from what Jesus was really trying to teach them. His concern was to focus on the heart of God illustrated by the man looking for his lost sheep, the woman searching for her lost coin and the father watching and waiting for the return of his lost boy and his merciful restoration of his wayward son.

Our focus, for purpose of this study, will be on the prodigal son. In studying his return and restoration as well as studying his older brother, we will glean much truth relating to our journey, not just from the pigpen home, but, as we shall see, from the servant's quarters back to the Father's house, to take our rightful place at His table.

The Younger Brother

Imagine yourself in the position of the young son. Having left home and having wasted all of his inheritance, he found himself hungry, penniless and friendless, doing something that no self-respecting Jewish boy should have been doing. He was tending pigs and, not being permitted to even eat the food that he is feeding to the pigs, he began to think back to his father's house.

Hunger can have a decidedly sobering effect upon a person's thinking. While he had plenty to eat, there was no desire to return to his father's house nor, probably, even to allow his mind to wander back to think of any benefit of being there. After all, that is why he had left home. To him home was obviously a symbol of restrictive control, a place that limited his ability to have fun.

Now, however, being in a place of deprivation, it was easy for him to think back to the abundance of the provision of his father's house and the freedom from lack that he enjoyed there. He could, no doubt, see himself sitting at the family table being served by the numerous servants in his father's employ, eating the nourishing food that was served in such an abundance, that there was always plenty left over.

No Longer a Son, But a Servant

The young man's reminiscing was suddenly interrupted by the realization that things could never be the same again. He could never return to his father's house as a son since he had taken his share of the inheritance prematurely. Technically, the father/son relationship had been terminated just as irrevocably as if a death had occurred.

Suddenly, a thought occurred to him that would change his life forever:

*"How many of my father's hired servants have bread enough **and to spare**, and I perish with hunger!"*

Luke 15:17

The advantages that his father's servants enjoyed over his present position were suddenly very obvious. Why should he be a hungry, destitute servant here in the far country when he could be a servant in his father's house? He could go home and ask his father to hire him as a servant. He would never ask for restoration to his position as a son, but he could beg his father for employment.

He began his long journey home rehearsing his speech of humiliation and supplication as he went:

"Father, I have sinned against heaven and before you, and am no longer worthy to be called your son.

Make me like one of your hired servants."

Luke 15:18-19

What a perfectly reasonable solution to his dilemma! He no longer need be hungry in this far country when he could be well fed as a servant in his father's house.

The Father's Love

The scene that he had rehearsed in his mind did not play out as he had imagined. The shame and remorse that he felt over his behavior (reflected in the speech he practiced as he walked) did not take the father's love into consideration. For all the time that his rebellious son has been away seeking an identity apart from his father and the family home, the father has been anxiously waiting and watching for his return. Many times the longing gaze of this devoted daddy had scanned the infinite depths of the horizon for the form of his lost boy whose gait he would immediately recognize.

None but those who have experienced the unconditional love and forgiveness of God our Father can grasp the tender compassion and all-covering mercy of the father as, without hesitation, he ran toward the far-off, broken figure of his boy. When he reached him, he did something that staggers the imagination. In our legalistic mindset, not understanding the mercy and loving-kindness of God, we would conceive of a cool reception with a strong look of disapproval and an emotional distance that would emphasize to the son the disgraceful behavior that he had been guilty of.

On Probation

How well I remember my own experience as a young boy. My father was a very strict disciplinarian who often disciplined me in anger and with tone of voice, words and facial expressions that were intended to convince me of the seriousness of my offense. The punishment was usually swift, severe, and often, in my perception, disproportionate to the offense. That would leave me with a profound sense of frustration, anger and hurt. The greatest frustration was what I perceived as a "cooling-off" period. A certain amount of time would have to pass before I felt accepted again by my father. That time span was undefined and arbitrary. I never knew how long it would take me to work my way back into Daddy's favor again and to feel approved, or more accurately, to feel less disapproved!

The effect of this perception of a cooling-off period with my father was that I projected the same concept into my relationship to God as Father. I lived in the feeling that, because of my sense of failure and sinfulness, I could never do enough to win God's approval. The immediate effect of falling into some specific sin was to feel totally rejected by God and unable to even come to Him in repentant prayer. I felt that there needed to be some undefined period of "cooling-off" until I felt better about myself before I could even go to God in prayer and repent of my sin and ask for His forgiveness. Often that period was marked by some compensatory behavior, some attempt at acts of righteousness that would impress God with the sincerity of my repentance. Try as I might, I could never feel that I had done enough nor was worthy enough of the Father's love.

The Power of Compassion

Our religious minds are scandalized by the father's action of running in abandoned joy and, with deep compassion stirring within him, throwing his arms around his boy and kissing him. The compassion that drove the father to such an extravagant act of mercy and unmerited favor must be a wonderful thing. What is it about compassion that enables a master to totally forgive an unworthy servant (Matthew 18:27), Jesus to interrupt his time of rest with His disciples to meet the needs of a selfish crowd (Mark 6:34), and the father to overlook the despicably self-centered behavior of this returning son? Notice in this story, as in many accounts relating to Jesus' ministry, the relationship between seeing

and compassion. Herein lies our problem. We see
through eyes jaundiced by our upbringing and personal woundedness, our religious ideas concerning
God, and our sense of justice based on an Old Covenant legalism. Because our God is a merciful God
whose heart is filled with love for those whom He
created, He looks at us with eyes that see, not our
unworthiness, sinfulness and the shame of our actions, but our deep hurt and need for acceptance,
forgiveness and love. When He sees us through
those merciful eyes, his compassion is triggered (the
Greek word used for compassion is, literally, 'lower
intestines' and is therefore translated in KJV
"bowels of mercy" in Colossians 3:12).

It is so difficult for many to conceive of God experiencing such kindly emotions. They are far more
comfortable with pictures of Him stirred with anger. That, in itself, is a reflection of their misunderstanding of His true nature. The Psalmist declared:

"The Lord is gracious and full of compassion,
Slow to anger and great in mercy."
                                          Psalm 145:8

Look with me again at the picture of the excited father running to his son, falling on his neck and kissing him. Such is the love and mercy of your heavenly
Father. Such is His unconditional love expressed in
receiving a wandering son home.

Beloved, it is time to lay down every wrong concept of the Father and to receive with joy the revelation of the Word that He **receives sinners and eats with them!** He is not holding you at arm's length in disapproval examining you minutely to find everything that is wrong with you. His arms are about you and, right now, He is planting a kiss right on your lips: a kiss of grace, a kiss of restoration and love. Don't reject His love as you continue to cling to a distorted image of what you conceive Him and religion has portrayed Him to be. He receives you and wants to eat with you, to enjoy the intimacy of the father/son or father/daughter relationship.

CHAPTER 7

The Blessings of the New Covenant

"But the father said to his servants, 'Bring out the best robe and put it on him, and put a ring on his hand and sandals on his feet. And bring the fatted calf here and kill it, and let us eat and be merry; for this my son was dead and is alive again; he was lost and is found.' And they began to be merry."

Luke 15:22-24

As I indicated in Chapter One, my personal pilgrimage from bondage into liberty has been a progressive appropriation of truth that has set me free from the deception of religion and legalism in which I grew up. As noted there, the theology that formed the basis for my father's preaching left me with uncertainty and doubt concerning my salvation and my ability to please God.

My experience can best be expressed in an observation made by a classmate to my daughter, Tracy, back in Junior High School. Though she was raised in a Christian home and was attending a Christian school, she chafed under the sometimes rigid attitudes that she encountered. One day, in a fit of frustration at a teacher's misguided effort to goad the young people to a higher standard of Christian living by laying the law on them, this young lady blurted out to Tracy, "You know, it's so hard to keep God happy!"

That about sums up the frustration that I lived in as I continually mourned my inability to live up to the standard of behavior I set for myself, a standard which, I believed, was what God expected of me. Associated with that, was the parallel fear of losing my salvation. My daddy's preaching had left me in no doubt that this was a distinct possibility if I was not living up to a standard that pleased God.

The fundamental paradigm shift that changed, not only my theological foundation, but also brought liberty to my oppressed soul, came through an understanding of the New Covenant. As much as I would love to, I cannot go into an extensive study of the New Covenant in this book. That must needs be the subject of another book. However, the covenantal aspects in this story of the father's love to his returning son will illuminate and illustrate the wonderful liberty that comes to a repentant child returning to God for forgiveness and restoration.

As the son began the speech that he had prepared, the father interrupted him by calling out to the servants:

"Bring out the best robe and put it on him, and put a ring on his hand and sandals on his feet. And bring

the fatted calf here and kill it, and let us eat and be
merry. "

Luke 15:22-23

Just As I Am

The father did not expect his son to do anything to
make himself ready to reenter the father's house.
He commanded the servants to bring out the best
robe, the ring, the sandals and the fatted calf to
where they were. The son had to go no further in
the state in which he had returned. What a wonderful picture of our Father's gracious love that uncon-
ditionally comes to where we are and changes us.
He takes the initiative to change us and forestalls
any attempt at self-improvement in order to come
into the Father's house. We come just as we are.

Bring Out The Best Robe

The robe that the father commanded the servants to
bring has wonderful application for us in our understanding of the position to which the Father exalts
us:

1. The robe is described as, literally in the Greek
   original, *"The robe, the best (or first) one."* This
   would not be just any garment. A robe was used
   as formal wear as opposed to daily attire. This

being the first or best one would indicate a robe reserved for very special occasions such as festivals and birthdays.

2. I believe the items of dress summoned by the father, as well as the killing of the fatted calf for a feast of celebration, have covenantal significance. In the making of covenants, there would be an exchange of gifts (often items of personal clothing such as a valuable robe), the slaughtering of an animal or shedding of blood by the parties involved and the sitting down to a feast to celebrate the making of covenant. Just as in the cutting of the Abrahamic covenant recorded in Genesis 15 where God's covenant-making was unilateral (He waited till Abraham was overcome with exhaustion and fell asleep), so here, because the son was regarded by the father as being *"dead,"* the action of the father was unilateral. The son could do nothing but receive, in childlike faith, the father's magnanimous gesture of restorative love.

3. The robe has a two-fold meaning in covenant making:

   a. The robe symbolizes life. An exchange of robe signifies the willingness of the two parties to lay down their lives for each other. An illustration of this can be found in the case of Jonathan and David (1 Samuel 18:4). Here, however, there was no exchange to one another. Certainly the son's dirty, smelly garment that represented his old life was removed from him to make way for the <u>best</u> robe and so reminds us of the re-clothing of Joshua the high priest in Zechariah 3:4. The father was giving the returning son his own life as a gift. He was received back, not with the life he once lived (of which he was now ashamed and from which he was turning), but with a new life imparted to him, the father's own life.

b. The robe also represents possessions. In covenantal terms, the one giving the robe was saying: "Everything I have now belongs to you. Whatever you may need, if I have it, it is yours. If ever you are in a situation of lack, all that I have is at your disposal. As long as I have possessions, you will never be in need." Though the son had taken his inheritance and squandered it and so had no legal claim to anything the father owned, the father was committing to his son, not a portion, but all that he had.

The Ring of Authority

The ring that the father called for is a wonderful picture of restored authority. The son had forfeited his position as a son and therefore his authority. The signet ring of the father placed on the son's finger would boldly declare the son's restored position as a member of the family, for that signet ring would carry the family seal. The gift of the ring was another covenant act of exchange. The son's forfeited rights were replaced by the imparted rights, not of a son, but the father's own authority.

The Sandals of Honor

The sandals are a symbol of the son's restored position. He had not been received back as a servant, but as an honored son. It was customary for slaves to go about their duties barefoot as a symbol of their position of servitude and subservience. The sandals given to the son were a mark of honor, a daily reminder that the father had not acquiesced to the son's desire to be hired as a servant.

The Fatted Calf

Now that the gifts have been given, the father called for the fatted calf to be killed so that by the shedding of blood, the covenant may be sealed and the celebratory feast prepared. The calf had been separated from the herd and given special food in order to prepare it for some unique occasion of celebration.

In the father's mind, no greater opportunity for

celebration can be found that would warrant the
slaying of the special animal. His son was dead but
now is alive. He was lost but now is found. What
cause for joyous celebration with feasting and
dancing!

"Bring the fatted calf here!" he called. He wanted
it slaughtered at the very spot in the road where he
had embraced the returning son. In the pouring out
of the calf's blood on the spot that marked such an
emotional restoration, a life was being given so that,
figuratively, from the blood-drenched dust, there
might emerge a new life for his son.

Our Position As Sons

Child of God, it is time for you to be confronted with
the position to which the Father has restored you.
The devil has for so long deceived us because of an
admixing of the Old Covenant with the New. As you
have been reading this chapter, I believe that there
has been a quickening in your heart as the implica-
tions of the father's restoration of the prodigal son
have begun to resonate in your spirit.

1. You are received unconditionally, just as you are

Think back to the moment when you came to God
as a sinner and invited Jesus into your heart. You,
too, came and were received just as you were. You

were not expected to change yourself as a prerequisite to being received back into the Father's house. How is it that we so easily listen to Satan's lies when he begins to lay on us condemnation and guilt and manipulates our emotions with feelings of unworthiness? Why do we then resort to compensatory behavior as we try to improve ourselves so that God will accept us and like us?

Like the prodigal son, when you came to the Father, He was waiting for you, not with words of rejection and condemnation. With merciful eyes, He had been watching for you. With a merciful heart, He ran to meet you on merciful feet. With merciful arms He embraced you, and, wonder of wonders, with merciful lips he kissed you with a kiss of forgiveness and grace. What love! No probationary period was prescribed for proving yourself truly repentant. No "cooling-off" period was required where the Father could work His way back to not feeling angry at you for your rebellious, sinful behavior. No! You were received with a genuine and wholehearted display of love, grace and mercy.

2. You are given a robe of righteousness, life and inheritance

The Father placed on you the robe of His righteousness. You never sit feasting at the Father's table in the robes of your own righteousness. However

beautiful they might appear to you, before Him they
are but filthy rags. No, He has stripped those gar-
ments from you and replaced them with the gor-
geous robe of His perfect righteousness. The reason that you are so freely received at the Father's
table is that whenever He looks at you, He sees you
covered with the robe of His own righteousness
which has been given to you through your faith in
Jesus Christ. Because the gift of righteousness has
now fitted you to stand unintimidated and
uncondemned before the Father, it is a gift of life.
You were once dead, but now you are alive again!
And there is more: that robe, representing all that
the Father has, marks you as an heir. All that the
Father has is now yours!

3. You have been given the ring of authority and dominion

Through Adam's sin, man has forfeited his position
of dominion and authority in this world. Through
Christ, the Anointed One, however, we have dominion and authority restored to us, not only over
all the works of God's hands, but also over the one
who usurped that authority, Satan, together with all
of his demonic hosts. It is for this very reason that
Satan does not want you to ever lose your sense of
unworthiness and guilt. As long as you feel con-
demned and unworthy, you will never be a match

for his powerful deception and intimidation. He knows exactly what button to push to vanquish a self-conscious Christian from the fight.

A rather humorous incident occurred many years ago when I was still coming out of a life of self-rejection and condemnation. I was attending a conference in Alabama where I was invited to preach. One evening, I was called to a room at the conference center where a young man was manifesting some demonic activity amongst much attention-getting behavior. When I arrived in the room, immediately I was deferred to, and began to take charge. I was very conscious of being about thirty pounds overweight at the time. After about twenty minutes of dealing with the situation in a somewhat ineffective way, I was getting frustrated in myself with my apparent lack of progress. Suddenly, the young man pointed at my stomach overhanging my belt and said: "Jelly-belly!" That did it! I was totally ineffective from that point on and soon slipped self-consciously out of the room!

There was no way that I could stand in authority over those demonic manifestations with such an awkward awareness of my own lack of spiritual discipline and self-control. Why? The answer is simply that I did not understand that I had my Father's ring on my finger. It was not my own ring. I was not coming in any authority based on personal piety, purity or prowess. No! It was through

His own authority given to me through Jesus Christ and exercised in Jesus' name! If I had been walking in the fullness of that revelation, I could have confidently asserted my authority and dominion over all the power of the devil and cast those lying, accusing demons out!

4. You have been given the sandals of honor

The cumulative evidence of the Scriptures that we have studied thus far is presented to settle forever in your spirit that you are not a servant but a son or a daughter of God. It is hardly likely that the prodigal son could ever overlook the significance of the robe and the ring. However, should he do so, there would always be the impact of the distinctive sandals which, every time he placed them on his feet, would remind him that his father had ignored his proposal to be made a servant and had marked him in this conspicuous fashion as a son.

Child of God, you have been marked by the Father by the gift of distinctive sandals.

"Stand therefore...having shod your feet with the preparation of the gospel of peace."
Ephesians 6:14-15

They are the sandals that provide a *"firm footing"* (the word translated *"preparation"* in the New King

James version of the Bible carries this meaning) given by the gospel of peace. What is your confidence and *"firm footing"* as a child of God? What gives you the right to walk confidently into the presence of the Father without any fear of rejection? It is simply this:

> *Therefore, having been justified by faith, we have peace with God through our Lord Jesus Christ, through whom also we have **access** by faith **into** this **grace** in which we **stand**, and rejoice in hope of the glory of God.*
>
> Romans 5:1-2

Look down at your sandals! They will declare the truth to you that you need to hear today. The good news is that there is peace in your relationship with God. He is no longer antagonistic toward you. He has been reconciled to you and has already reconciled you to Himself in Jesus Christ (2 Corinthians 5:18-19). Receive that truth today. By faith step over into the firm footing of grace and stand unintimidated by the accuser of your soul and begin to rejoice in hope! Rejoice! You are accepted! You are forgiven! You are loved! Welcome home, "Son!"

CHAPTER 8

The Older Brother

"Now his older son was in the field. And as he came and drew near to the house, he heard music and dancing. So he called one of the servants and asked what these things meant. And he said to him, 'Your brother has come, and because he has received him safe and sound, your father has killed the fatted calf.' But he was angry and would not go in. Therefore his father came out and pleaded with him. So he answered and said to his father, 'Lo, these many years I have been serving you; I never transgressed your commandment at any time; and yet you never gave me a young goat, that I might make merry with my friends. But as soon as this son of yours came, who has devoured your livelihood with harlots, you killed the fatted calf for him.'"

Luke 15:25-30

In responding to the criticism of the scribes and Pharisees, Jesus has given us a glorious insight into the nature of God as father and into His gracious dealing with sinful man. In doing so, He has given an explanation as to why He could so freely associate with people with whom the religious leaders of the day disdained to have any association. Now Jesus is about to expose these religious leaders and the curse of religion itself. In the part of the parable that details the reaction of the older brother, Jesus is about to give the clearest insight in the Bible into the awful curse of religious blindness. He is about to expose the class of people who cannot rejoice when a lost sheep, a lost coin or a lost son are found.

Religious Blindness

The great tragedy in this parable is the blindness of the older brother. Although he has lived with his father for all these years, he does not really know him. His shocked and angry reaction to his father's expression of mercy and love to his younger brother is typical of the religious mindset that Jesus battled throughout His entire ministry. In fact, it was that mindset in the religious leaders that caused them to be offended at the way He apparently snubbed His nose at their religious traditions. Ultimately, it led them, in jealous anger, to demand His death.

"I Desire Mercy and Not Sacrifice"

Jesus confronted this religious blindness with a statement that is most offensive to those with a religious mindset. We will identify this mindset as an "older-brother mentality."

Two illustrations in Matthew's gospel serve to reveal to us the gross ignorance of the character of God displayed by both the Pharisees and the older brother, and which is typical of the older-brother mentality.

When Jesus called Matthew, who himself was a much-despised tax collector, it seems that Matthew immediately invited Jesus to a meal at his home (see Matthew 9:9-13). To the consternation and chagrin of the Pharisees, *"many tax collectors and sinners came and sat down with Him and His disciples,"* (Verse 10). That was obviously a great vexation to the Pharisees because, in the tradition of the elders, such association would make a Jew ceremonially unclean. What is more, since a man is known by the company he keeps, then Jesus must have some flaw in His character to associate with such a group.

In the second incident, Jesus was walking with his hungry disciples through the grainfields (see Matthew 12:1-8). His disciples began to pick heads of grain and eat them. There is nothing wrong with that, is there? The problem was, it was the Sabbath. By picking grain, which would be classified as work, they were violating the Sabbath laws. In fact, their being in the field was probably also a violation of the Sabbath travel laws.

Suddenly, from among the surrounding grain stalks, the Pharisees popped up. What were they doing there? Obviously, their only reason for being there was to find fault with Jesus. In response to both of these incidents, Jesus gave the same quotation from Hosea:

"I desire mercy and not sacrifice."

Hosea 6:6

Hosea was expressing God's reaction to cold, dead formalism that goes through the requirements of the ritual law without heartfelt worship. In that verse, God went on to say: *"...and the knowledge of God more than burnt offerings."* Herein lay the great tragedy in the religious fervor of the Pharisees. While pursuing a rigid keeping of the external demands of the Law, the traditions of the elders, and the Levitical sacrificial system, they had not come to know the true nature of God.

In a similar way, the older brother's perception of his father was completely wrong. He said: *"Lo, these many years I have been serving you; I never transgressed your commandment at any time"* (Luke 15:29). He saw his father as a man who demanded perfect obedience to his commandments and faultless execution of all of his requirements. The son saw his father not as a merciful, loving father but as an onerous master. His perception determined his behavior. He perfectly served his father as a master rather than knowing and enjoying him intimately as a father.

More than that, this perception limited his father's relationship to him. Since he perceived his father as a master and himself as a servant, the father had, apparently, never been able to elevate the relationship beyond that. In spite of living in the father's house for all these years, his blindness, caused by his perception of his father, had held the father at bay. The resulting mental and emotional barrier had never allowed the father to press through and show him the depth of emotional love that he poured out on the prodigal son. That was why the father's display of extravagant love and grace came as such a shock to him. His mistaken understanding of his father's nature prohibited his father from being to him more than his distorted concept allowed.

Out of Our Own Mouths We Are Judged

This concept is most challengingly set forth in the parable of the talents found in Matthew 25:

> *"Then he who had received the one talent came and said, 'Lord, I **knew** you to be a hard man, reaping where you have not sown and gathering where you have not scattered seed. And I was afraid.'"*
>
> Matthew 25:24-25

The servant's perception of his master was completely faulty. He believed that the master reaped where he had not sown. However, Jesus clearly set out the master's requirement:

> *"So you ought to have deposited **my** money with the bankers, and at **my** coming I would have received back **my own** with interest."*
>
> Matthew 25:27

The master did not expect anything more than what he had given to the servant and the increase that it, not the servant, was able to produce. He had provided the seed. The increase was not dependent on the servant's ability but on the power of the seed to reproduce itself if placed in the bank. From Jesus' own words it is clear that this was not an accurate perception of the master's character. He was not a *"hard man."* He did not *"gather"* where he had *"not scattered seed,"* as the servant perceived.

However faulty the man's belief was, it determined his action. More alarmingly, it determined the master's response to him:

> *"'For I feared you, because you are an austere man.'*
> *And he said to him, '**Out of your own mouth I will judge you...**'"*
>
> Luke 19:21-22

The master then proceeded to confirm the servant's assessment of him: *"You knew that I was an austere man, collecting what I did not deposit and reaping what I did not sow,"* (verse 22). That this was not an accurate assessment of the master is made clear by his own words: *"my money"* and *"I would have received back my own with interest"* (Matthew 25:27). What Jesus was showing us was that the master was bound by what the servant believed and confessed him to be. *"Out of your own mouth I will judge you,"* the master exclaimed.

What we believe in our hearts will determine, both our actions, and the confession out of our mouths. What comes out of our mouths, being an expression of the belief of our hearts, will determine God's basis for relating to us. It becomes soberingly clear that God can be no more to us than we believe, confess and receive Him to be. The fundamental principle that determines our relationship to God and what we receive from Him and what He can be to us, is enunciated by Jesus over and over again during His ministry: *"As you have believed so let it be done for you"* (Matthew 8:13), and again, *"According to your faith let it be to you"* (Matthew 9:29).

Just like the servant in the parables of the talents and pounds, the older brother was cursed by his wrong belief. He had a wrong perception of the character of his father reflected in the words that came out of his mouth. He perceived his father as a stern, austere master who was difficult to please and who did not easily reward diligent service and exemplary behavior. Notice his accusation directed at his father's apparent stinginess and failure to recognize and reward his diligent service and perfect obedience:

> *"Lo, these many years I have been serving you; I have never transgressed your commandment at any time; and yet you never gave me a young goat, that I might make merry with my friends."*
>
> Luke 15:29

In comparison with his father's apparent lack of generosity toward him, he saw his father extravagantly endowing his younger brother. The seething anger that erupted as he considered this partial and unfair treatment blinded his eyes to the amazing revelation of the father's true nature unfolding in the welcome to the lost brother.

In the next chapter we are going to explore in greater depth the older brother's perception of himself in relationship to the father. But before we pursue that line of study, it is imperative that we recognize that our perception of the Father determines our perception of ourselves. Just like the older brother, who is a reflection of the scribes and Pharisees to whom Jesus is addressing this story, we will perceive ourselves wrongly if we have a wrong concept of the Father.

Jesus Reveals the True Nature of the Father

The Pharisees and scribes claimed to be the ones who had the true knowledge of God. Through this account of the older brother and his reaction, both to the prodigal's return and to the father's unconditional, extravagant reception of him, Jesus was revealing to them their utter ignorance of God as Father.

Through the law, God was revealed as a demanding, austere God who could not tolerate failure and disobedience. His holiness was revealed as being unable to have any contact with sinful, unbelieving man. But that was not the complete revelation of God in the Word. His mercy provided a sacrificial system under that same law that foreshadowed a perfect redemptive sacrifice that would open the way into His presence. The prophets foretold a new covenant that God would make by which man would be able to draw near to God through His mercy and grace.

Now Jesus was in the world to unveil the true nature of God the Father. The religious leaders, who should have understood, were unable to grasp this reckless display, not only of tolerance for sinners, but also of an acceptance that permitted intimate fellowship. They were incensed, instead of being delighted, at this display of compassion, mercy and love.

Child of God, let me challenge your perception of God as Father. Jesus has come into the world to reveal the Father to man. He could say, *"He who has seen me has seen the Father"* (John 14:9). The testimony of Hebrews 1:3 confirms this: *"Who being the brightness of His glory and the **express image** of His person."* In spite of this, many still live with a false dichotomy between the Father whom Jesus reveals and the God revealed in the law. Many Christians still differentiate between a holy God who is so pure that He cannot look upon iniquity and Jesus who came and actually ate with sinners. We are unable to see the two as one because of our ignorance of the New Covenant, the true nature of Father-God, and our tendency to mix the Old Covenant into the New.

The Father loves you, receives you and wants to have intimate communion with you. He desires to break through your confused perception of Himself and reveal His Fatherly love and goodness to you. Do not let the tragedy of the older brother befall you. He never knew his own father even though he had lived under the same roof with him for all those years. How sad that so many have lived 'under the Father's roof' for many years and yet have never really known His true nature of love.

Jesus sent the Holy Spirit in His place to continue the revealing process in us. Right now ask the Holy Spirit to open the eyes of your heart to the revelation of the Father in Jesus the Anointed One and allow the truth to set you free. Allow the Father to embrace you and prepare the feast of celebration as He welcomes you home. I invite you to pray this prayer right now:

"Father, I repent of wrong concepts of who You are. Like the older brother, I am Your child and yet have related to You as a servant to a master. Because of religious tradition and childhood upbringing, my concept of your Fatherhood has been wrong in many respects. Holy Spirit, I receive you as the Spirit of revelation. Please reveal the Father to me as Jesus came to reveal the Father. Heal my broken heart through which the truth of Your Word has been distorted. Open the eyes of my heart to know God as the merciful, loving, generous Father Jesus revealed Him to be.

I ask this in the name of Jesus the Anointed One who by His anointing came to set captives free."

Amen!

CHAPTER 9

The Mentality of a Servant

"So he answered and said to his father, 'Lo, these many years I have been serving you; I never transgressed your commandment at any time; and yet you never gave me a young goat, that I might make merry with my friends. But as soon as this son of yours came, who has devoured your livelihood with harlots, you killed the fatted calf for him.'"
                                                    Luke 15:29-30

"Yes, Sir." "No thank you, Ma'am." When we immigrated to the United States in 1982, it was a major culture shock to hear children address their parents in such a formal way! I had grown up with the intimate form of address of 'Daddy' and 'Mommy.' Bev and I did not want our children to adapt to, what seemed to us, a strange method of addressing parents.

I firmly resisted the pressure placed on Tracy and Bradley from outside the home to conform to this new custom. They should, by all means, use such an address for other adults. However, we insisted that they called us "Mommy" and "Daddy." I did not want my children to address us as though we were their masters.

Now I understand that this is a cultural thing and have no desire to offend anyone. However, I perceive a problem here. In our attempt to train children to respect their parents, we have helped perpetuate the unfortunate perception of parents as masters who are to be obeyed. Our culture is cursed with a performance mindset that permeates education, athletics and, sadly, the parent/child relationship. Is it any wonder then that so many Christians have such difficulty in viewing God as Father according to Biblical revelation? Like the older brother, they perceive God as a Master to be perfectly obeyed and diligently served rather than as a Father with whom intimate relationship is possible.

Your Perception of God Determines Your Self-Concept

The result of this distorted perception of God is a distorted self-perception. If God is nothing more than a Master to be served and obeyed, then we become mere servants. Our focus then as believers is on finding commandments to obey and duties to perform and fulfilling them to the best of our abilities.

That is how the older brother saw himself. A servant! Although he had lived under the same roof as this loving, merciful man, he had never seen him as anything other than a master to be obeyed and therefore himself as a servant living on a performance standard.

This son had maintained a high standard. Consider his self-evaluation: *"Lo, these many years I have been serving you; I never transgressed your commandment at any time"* (Luke 15:29). What a lofty standard he had maintained throughout his life! He could look back on a life of perfect obedience. Like the rich young ruler and the Apostle Paul, he had a perfect record of obedience. The rich young ruler could say:

"All these things I have kept from my youth."

Luke 18:21

Paul, in recounting all the advantages and achievements that were his before coming to Christ, said of himself:

"Concerning the righteousness which is in the law, blameless."

Philippians 3:6

In each of these three cases, the trust of these men was in their perfect performance of requirements. In all cases, rather than their trust being in the nature and character of God (in the case of the older brother, his father), their confidence was in their blameless record. Surely that would be recognized! Surely that would be rewarded!

Imagine the deep hurt, the confusion, the anger when
the older brother heard the servant tell of the extravagance of the father's love toward the young brother.
The greatest offense of the father's mercy was his
generosity to an undeserving son who had squandered
his inheritance on loose living.

A Skinny Goat Vs. A Fatted Calf

We are now coming to the heart of the difference
between a servant and a son. Jesus' story-telling is
brilliant. What an offense! The father has killed
the fatted calf to celebrate the younger brother's
return. In all probability, the older brother himself
had been entrusted with the special care of this calf.
Day after day he had diligently given it the extra
nutrition to fatten it up to the point that it would be
ready for a festive occasion. He had possibly day-
dreamed of the day when, in recognition of his exemplary behavior, his father would give him that very
calf to have a feast with his friends.
Consider again the angry sarcasm of the son:

> *"Yet you never gave me a young goat, that I might
> make merry with my friends."*   Verse 29

The Greek word for goat is "eriphon." Some manuscripts use the diminutive form of the word,
"eriphion." The New King James Version of the

Bible translates it as *'young goat.'* The word literally means *"tiny goat"* or *"skinny goat."* I believe
the latter translation to better reflect the livid sarcasm in the older brother. The comparison is so
obvious! The father killed the fatted calf for his
younger brother but had never even given him a
tiny, skinny goat. How unfair!

Here is the classic dilemma of the legalist who
cannot grasp the superiority of mercy over justice.
Jesus had told the Pharisees: *"But go and learn
what this means; 'I desire mercy and not sacrifice"*
(Matthew 9:13). In the Pharisees' mind, there was
no way that mercy was superior to sacrifice.

James, in summarizing his discourse on partiality
and judgmentalism, declared: *"For judgment is without mercy to the one who has shown no mercy. Mercy
triumphs over judgment"* (James 2:13). This last
phrase can best be translated: *"Mercy is superior
to justice."*

The Legalist

The preoccupation of the legalist is the minutiae of
the requirements of the law. The Pharisees and
scribes were so intent on doing everything that the
law demanded that they completely overlooked the
true nature of God. They related to God on a basis
of justice based on their pursuit of personal
righteousness. If they perfectly fulfilled all the re-

quirements, then God, in his justice, would reward them accordingly.

Here are some of the characteristics of a legalist:

1. A legalist is one who lives his life regulated by laws and rules.
2. The goal of a legalist is flawless compliance with every rule that he believes applicable.
3. A legalist believes that acceptance by God is dependent upon perfect conformity to all the laws, ordinances and precepts laid out in the Bible.
4. A legalist is hard on himself but at the same time covers his failure to live up to the standard he sets himself by a hypocritical outward show of piety.
5. A legalist compares his performance to that of others around him and is either puffed up with pride or driven to despair because he perceives others as better than himself.
6. A legalist is extremely judgmental of others around him for, in finding fault with them, it makes him feel better about himself and his own performance.
7. The goal of a legalist in his life of rigid discipline, self-denial and finicky perfectionism is to earn a reward from God.
8. When God fails to reward a legalist according to his expectation, and when he perceives God acting unfairly toward those whom he considers undeserving, he is angry and offended.

The older brother, with his servant mentality, portrayed many of these characteristics. His blindness to the true nature of his father also distorted his perception of his relationship to his father. He was totally blind to all the benefits of living in his father's home. Only one thing consumed him. The prize! The reward! Having served the father so diligently and obeyed him perfectly, surely now the father would reward him accordingly. Instead, the brother is horrified, perplexed and angered when the father blesses the young son upon his return.

I recently heard a similar story of a businessman who had brought his older son into the family business. This son through hard work and astute business dealings had helped the father build the family business up into a multi-million-dollar empire. The youngest son had never been interested in the family business and had gone his own way to sow his wild oats. After many years of irresponsible, reckless living and alienation from the family, a radical change had occurred in the young son which had led to reconciliation and restoration with his father.

The father, overjoyed at the return of his prodigal son, had proceeded to bring him into the business as a full partner with his hard-working brother. You can imagine the reaction! Suddenly the older brother had to deal with all sorts of emotions as he attempted to deal with the father's loving generosity on the one hand, and apparent lack of appreciation for his faithfulness, stability and diligence, on the other.

Not a Reward – An Inheritance

Now we are coming to the crux of the servant/son dilemma. At issue is the skinny goat. Why did the father not reward the older brother for his long years of diligent service? The answer to that question contains one of the most important truths that you will read in this book:

It was impossible for the father to reward the son with that which already belonged to him by inheritance!

All the skinny goats and fatted calves already belonged to him, for he was a son and therefore an heir! He could have had a party every day of his life. The father said to him: *"All that I have is yours"* (Verse 31).

What a tragedy! Since the older brother perceived himself as a servant rather than a son, he awaited a reward and forfeited the enjoyment of his inheritance. Everything his father had was his by inheritance, but he could never receive what rightfully was his to enjoy. His servant mentality limited him to the anticipation of a wage or reward and kept him from recognizing his liberty as an heir to appropriate what was his.

Why is it that so many believers cannot receive their healing? Why is it that so many Christians live in poverty? Why do so many godly people live in such fear and lack of assurance? Why do earnest Christians who desire everything that God has for them never receive the blessings promised in the Word? The answer is so clear. They are waiting for a reward and, because they are heirs, the Father can never give them, as a reward, what already belongs to them.

The Gifts of the Spirit

Let me use an example. I have heard many Christians say (and I have been guilty of saying in the past) words to this effect: "Well, I believe in all the gifts of the Spirit. I am open to whatever God has for me. I desire spiritual gifts, and I am open to receive the gift of tongues, but God just has not given me that gift. I guess I will just have to wait until God is ready to give that gift to me. He must know that I am not ready to receive it yet."

Do you see the flaw in such thinking? All the gifts of God to us are promised gifts of the new covenant, which are secured by the death of Jesus on the cross and available to us through the ministry of the Holy Spirit. They are already ours! When we believe the truth of who we are as sons and daughters and therefore heirs, we will in simple faith receive what

already belongs to us. Many have been confused by
Paul's teaching in 1 Corinthians 12 on manifestations of the Spirit which are applied, in context, to
"When you come together," (11:33, 14:26). In that
context of the gathered community of believers, the
Holy Spirit manifests Himself *"as He wills,"* (12:11).
However, Paul exhorts the Corinthians, and us, to
"desire (literally, "to burn with desire") *spiritual
gifts, but especially that you may prophesy,"* (14:1).
God wants us to enjoy the benefit and blessing of
what is ours by birthright as His sons and daughters. When you desire spiritual gifts and recognize
their importance to your personal walk and your
ministry, you will receive them, not as a reward,
but as a free gift.

Peace Is a Gift

Many forfeit the enjoyment of peace with God for
the same reason. Because they see righteousness as
a reward for perfect performance, they are waiting
for God to reward them with a sense of peace and
well-being as a manifestation of his pleasure with
them and acceptance of them. God cannot do that.
Peace is a fruit of the Spirit (see Galatians 5:22)
bequeathed to us by Jesus. He said:

"Peace I leave with you."   John 14:27

God's peace is given to us on the basis of justification by faith. Paul taught:

"Therefore, having been justified by faith, we have peace with God through our Lord Jesus Christ."

Romans 5:1

Under the New Covenant, peace is never a reward for perfect obedience and diligent service. It is an inherited gift.

It is time for you, child of God, to come out of that servant mentality that has driven you to perform and then wait for a reward from the Father, and to enter into your inheritance as a son and daughter. It is time for you to get angry with the deception of Satan working through confused teaching and preaching and press into knowing the truth about who you are as an heir of God and all the inheritance that He has already covenanted to you.

In the following chapters we will look at three of the most troubling areas of failure on the part of many believers to receive their inheritance: healing, intimacy and prosperity.

CHAPTER 10

The Children's Bread

"From there He arose and went to the region of Tyre and Sidon. And he entered a house and wanted no one to know it. But He could not be hidden. For a woman whose young daughter had an unclean spirit heard about Him, and she came and fell at His feet. The woman was a Greek, a Syro-Phoenecian by birth, and she kept asking Him to cast the demon out of her daughter. But Jesus said to her, 'Let the children be filled first, for it is not good to take the children's bread and throw it to the little dogs.'"

Mark 7:24-27

At first reading, this event in Jesus' earthly ministry appears so hard to understand, particularly in the light of what we have seen of the Father's merciful character. If Jesus has come to reveal the true nature of the Father, does this not seem incongruous for Him to treat this woman with apparent harshness and insensitivity?

No. What we have here is a wonderful revelation of the covenant-keeping faithfulness of God to His children. Jesus regarded the deliverance for which this Greek woman was asking as bread reserved for children.

What Is the Children's Bread?

There is an expression in our language that I grew up with: Bread is the staff of life. We mean by this that it is a basic necessity to sustain life. It is also a basic right of a child in the home. Parents are responsible to provide basic necessities for the sustenance of the lives of their children.

Some have limited the application of this truth only to the deliverance from demonization referred to in this story. That, I believe, is far too limiting. It is clear that Jesus' ministry encompassed many whose needs were not pure demonizations but which the Holy Spirit, through Peter, classifies as an oppression of the Devil:

"How God anointed Jesus of Nazareth with the Holy Spirit and with power, who went about doing good and healing all who were oppressed by the devil, for God was with Him."   Acts 10:38

It is clear from Isaiah 61:1-3, the wonderful prophecy concerning the Anointed One and His anointing, that the anointing deals with more than deliverance from demonization. Included in the promised ministry of the Anointed One are the poor, the broken-hearted, captives, mourners as well as those to whom a declaration of "Jubilee" would be good news: the disenfranchised, those in debt, etc. Since Peter regarded the anointing as God's provision operating in Jesus to heal *"all who were oppressed by the devil,"* then we may rightly regard *"the children's bread"* as being the entire ministry of Jesus by the anointing. Included, then, would be preaching good news to the poor (prosperity), healing for the broken hearted (or emotional healing) and the physical healing obviously included by Peter in Acts 10:38.

Why would this be called *"the children's bread?"* To answer this question, we need to consider another event in Jesus' ministry.

"Woman, You are Loosed"

*"Now He was teaching in one of the synagogues on the Sabbath. And behold, there was a woman who had a spirit of infirmity eighteen years, and was bent over and could in no way raise herself up. But when Jesus saw her, He called her to Him and said to her, "Woman, you **are loosed** from your infirmity." And He laid His hands on her, and immediately she was made straight, and glorified God. But the ruler of the synagogue answered with indignation.... The Lord then answered him and said, 'Hypocrite...So ought not this woman, being a **daughter of Abraham**, who Satan has bound (think of it) for eighteen years, be loosed from this bond on the Sabbath?'"*

Luke 13:10-16

I believe with all of my heart that if we could only grasp the significance of Jesus words in this story, there would not be a single believer not pressing in to obtain, in simple faith, healing, deliverance and everything else that is theirs by inheritance. In order to grasp the profound significance of what Jesus said and did in this account, let me do a little Greek grammar study with you.

The Greek Perfect Tense

The perfect tense of the verb in Greek is different from the perfect tense in English. In the Greek perfect tense, the emphasis of the verb is on a state of being which has resulted from a past action. While the past action is obviously called to mind, it is not the focus of the verb. Let me use a simple example. We say in English, "I am married." That statement assumes that a marriage ceremony took place in the past but the focus is on the resultant state of being. "I am married now." That is my present condition. It is not something that I hope will come about in the future. It is reality now. In my case a ceremony took place in East London, South Africa on January 20, 1973 where I took Beverley Wegener to be my wife. The Aorist Tense would be used in Greek to describe that past event. However we remain married now and only occasionally do we recall the ceremony. The focus of our lives is on the state of marriage that we are in.

You Are Loosed By a Covenant

Where are we going with all of this? I have given this explanation since, I believe, it is vital to understand the implication of the words that Jesus used. When Jesus said to the woman, *"You are loosed,"* He used the perfect tense. In other words, He was inferring that something had happened before this occasion that had loosed her from her infirmity and left her in a state of being loosed. "But," some may say, "she was still bound by that infirmity until Jesus touched her." Wrong! According to Jesus, something had already taken place that had completely liberated her and healed her from this sickness which Jesus classified as an oppression and bondage of Satan.

What was the event that was called to mind by Jesus use of the perfect tense? The answer is apparent in Jesus' own words. He referred to this woman as *"a daughter of Abraham."* She was the offspring or seed of Abraham and was therefore entitled to all the blessings and benefits promised to Abraham and guaranteed by God's unilateral cutting of covenant with Abraham (see Genesis 15). These blessings were not dependent on performance for they were given by a promise. They were simply to be received by faith, just as Abraham received them and was accounted as righteous by God.

What Jesus was saying was that this woman was loosed back there under that starry sky when God

made the promise to Abraham and then sealed that
covenant promise by passing through the spread pieces
of the animals while Abraham slept. That was the
night of her deliverance, thousands of years before.
That is why Jesus could declare her *"loosed"* when
physically she was still bent over and unable to raise
herself up. The declaration of truth preceded the
appropriation of the covenant blessing.

"All That I Have Is Yours"

The older brother was in the same position. The
father said to him, *"All that I have is yours."* The
son was whining about not getting some skinny goat.
He had it all, but he didn't have it. He possessed it
all but had never appropriated any of it. By right of
inheritance, he owned all that his father had, but had
never been able to get past his servant-mentality and
receive what belonged to him.

Notice the sequence of events in the healing of the
woman. Jesus declared what He knew to be the truth.
Healing was a settled issue. That is why He had
come. As the *"messenger of the covenant"* (Malachi
3:1), He had come to declare what Abraham's descendants had a right to enjoy but were forfeiting by ignorance. He has no doubt that, when He laid His hands on
this woman, the healing would be manifested. It was a
done deal! Healing cannot fail to be manifested
since it took place when the covenant was cut.

Is Healing In the Atonement?

The lengths to which some theologians will go to try
to prove that healing is not in the atonement are ludi-
crous. The question is moot. Healing **is** in the covenant, firstly with Abraham, and then in the new covenant sealed in Jesus blood:

*"And if you are Christ's, then you are Abraham's seed,
and heirs according to the promise."*

Galatians 3:29

For those of us who are not only the seed of Abraham
but also heirs of God through Christ, the promises
of God are guaranteed. Paul wrote:

*"For all the promises of God in Him are Yes, and in
Him Amen, to the glory of God through us. Now He
who establishes us with you in Christ [the Anointed
one] and has anointed us is God, who also has sealed
us and given us the Spirit in our hearts as a
guarantee."*

2 Corinthians 1:20-22

Note the following in reference to this verse:

1. Jesus, as the seed of Abraham, is the One who
   confirms **all** the promises of God on our behalf
   and for our benefit.

2. Those promises are the basis of our confidence and produce stability and assurance in the believer.

3. That stability is in Christ, the Anointed One. The reality of His anointing and what that anointing accomplishes, give us the confidence to expect fulfillment of every promise.

4. The same anointing that operated in Jesus is upon us now. The same things that Jesus accomplished by the anointing in fulfillment of the promises of the Father can be accomplished **in** and **through** every believer.

5. God receives glory when His promises are fulfilled in us.

6. The Holy Spirit within us is the seal of every covenant promise to us and the guarantee that when we come in faith to appropriate our promised inheritance, we will never be denied.

A Basic Necessity

It is clear from Jesus' words and ministry that He regarded healing not as an optional extra but as *"the children's bread,"* a basic necessity. He is unequivocal in asserting the right of the crippled woman to be loosed from her infirmity as a daughter of Abraham. What does this mean for us today?

It is so sad to see so many Christian's living with

sickness, disease and infirmity. Your birthright as a
child of the Father is to be well. In fact, you are
already well! When God cut covenant with Abraham
you were loosed from all infirmity. Why do we not
then appropriate our healing?

1. The Fear of Ridicule:

There has been a vigorous attack on the idea of
confessing something to be true when it, apparently, is not so. People who confess that they are
well when they are obviously still sick have been
so ridiculed that it has produced a fear in many
Christians. We are afraid of being labeled as "un-
realistic" or worse.

Our problem is that we have not been able to differentiate between truth and fact. The truth is that
we **are** loosed from our infirmity. The fact might
be that we are still physically displaying symptoms
of a disease. By confessing the fact, "I am sick,"
we will never progress into healing. As we have
seen, Jesus declared the woman loosed (in fact,
loosed thousands of years before) when she was still
bent over with her crippling infirmity.

We have to begin to declare, not the fact of our
present condition as it appears, but the truth of our
present condition based on the covenant and the promises of God. If the Bible says, *"By whose stripes
you were healed"* (1 Peter 2:24), since, in Peter's

view, the healing took place when Jesus was stripped
bare and beaten over his back till stripes appeared,
then it is imperative that I say, "By the stripes of
Jesus I am healed!" Only then will the facts begin to
change to conform to the truth that I am confessing.
Do not be intimidated by some religious people, bound
by unbelief, who make fun of those who have learned
to confess the truth of the Word. You have Jesus as
your example, so go for it! Begin to confess the truth,
"I am loosed from my infirmity. I am healed." Do
not become weary in sowing those seeds of truth into
the soil of your heart through the confession of your
mouth. God's promise is: *"In due season we shall
reap if we do not lose heart"* (Galatians 6:9).

2. The Servant Mentality:

Probably the greatest hindrance to healing is the lin-
gering servant mentality that shapes the thinking of
so many Christians. It manifests itself in a number
of ways:

a. A groveling unworthiness that does not allow us
   to feel worthy enough to be rewarded with
   healing.
b. A frustration in that God does not seem to reward
   all of our diligent, loyal service, all of our
   prayers and fasting with the desired healing.

When people come during ministry time requesting
healing, I often ask them: "Do you believe God
will heal you?" Many times they respond with
statements of how long they have served the Lord,
how much they have prayed for healing (and been
prayed for), how faithful they are in their local
church, etc.

c. An inner drive to do more to impress God with
   our sincerity, diligence and faith.
d. A settling for sickness as our lot in life, the cross
   we have to bear, and a mistaken idea that God is
   using the sickness to, at best, teach them
   something and, at worst, to punish them. The
   scripture is clear on both of these assumptions:

   i. God teaches us by His word and His Spirit, not
      by something for which Jesus died on the cross.
   ii. Since Jesus has taken our punishment upon
       himself, God could never place on my body
       what was carried by Jesus in His body on the
       cross.

Identifying A Servant Mentality

How can we determine if we are still coming as a
servant to receive our healing? There is a simple
way. If, when healing does not manifest we lapse
into self-evaluation of whether we prayed right,

confessed correctly or spoke the correct healing 'formula,' we can be sure that we came as a servant. In other words our trust was in **how we came to God** and in our performance, not on the character, promise and faithfulness of God.

It has been such a joy for Bev and me to see how many people are able to receive their healing when we teach and preach on sonship in this way. When God's children finally accept who they are as sons and daughters, many are able to step over into simple faith and appropriate what is theirs by covenant.

Child of God, healing is (amongst many other things) *"the children's bread."* It is not the children's cake! It is your right and privilege as a child of God, a seed of Abraham. It is time for you to begin to declare boldly and unrelentingly until the fact becomes conformed to the truth: "I am loosed from my infirmity! I am healed by the stripes of Jesus! A covenant was made and blood was shed so that I might be freed from this oppression of the devil. I will not dishonor the parties to that covenant, and the precious blood that was shed to confirm it, by confessing what I see with my eyes, or feel in my body, one more time! I am healed! Hallelujah!"

If you will do that, you will see the manifestation of what God promised to Abraham so many years ago. You will be blessed with the children's bread.

CHAPTER 11

The Birthright of Sons: Intimacy

"And he said to him, 'Son, you are always with me, and all that I have is yours.'"　　　　　Luke 15:31

It is mind-boggling to try to imagine how much the older brother forfeited as a result of his servant mentality. Think of all those times when he could have taken a calf from his daddy's herd and had the servants prepare a feast for him and his friends. Think of the daily grind of duties that he performed hoping to be noticed by his father and rewarded accordingly. Think of the joy that he could have experienced in pressing in to know his daddy and the obvious depths of love, favor and generosity that would have enriched, reassured and blessed him.

Instead, we see an angry, bitter man who never came to know his father and lived imprisoned in a system of justice and fairness that never seemed to lean toward his benefit. We see a legalist blinded by his sense of justice and cheated out of his birthright as the eldest son by the shackles of a servant mentality. We see an uptight performer continually frustrated out of his sought-after reward by the apparent unfairness of a father who seemed not to notice how hard he was trying. What we have here is a poster boy for twentieth century "saved-to-serve" Christianity at its religious, legalistic worst!

The most powerful statement of the covenant rights of every believer is made in this passage from Luke 15. In it, the father stated, in essence, what are the two fundamental birthrights of a son or daughter of Father God.   There are many other rights but they are all encompassed in the two rights stated by the father. We will study the first in this chapter

Uninterrupted Intimacy and Fellowship

What wonderful words Jesus placed in the father's mouth! What a grand revelation we are given as the father answered, *"Son!"* Though the older brother saw himself as a servant with the responsibility of perfect obedience and impeccable service, the father called him a son. Oh, how we need the Spirit of sonship who indwelt Jesus to boom into the darkest recesses of our innermost being with that affirmation: *"Son!"* How much we need Him to destroy that *"high thing"* of a servant mentality that *"exalts itself against the knowledge of God"* (2 Corinthians 10:5). That reasoning or *"argument,"* as the New King James Version of the Bible translates it (literally, it means "a system of thought"), needs to be destroyed by the truth of what God has redeemed us to be. We are not servants. We are His sons and daughters!

Teknon, Not *Huios*

In addressing the older brother as *'son,'* Jesus did not use the usual Greek word *huios*. Rather he used the word *teknon*. The significance of this choice of word is powerful. Had he used the word *huios*, Jesus would have been emphasizing the nature of the relationship between the father and his son. It could be used of an adopted son. In every other place where *"son"* is used in this story, this is the Greek word that is utilized. Why does Jesus change the word now?

The word *teknon* is derived from the word *tikto* which means "to beget, bring forth or bear" a child. The emphasis of this word is not on the nature of the relationship. He could not use this word for the younger brother because technically he was dead, as the father declared in verse 24. No longer did his natural birth have any bearing on the relationship. He was restored to the relationship of sonship by the mercy of the father and through the covenant symbols, especially through the shed blood of the fatted calf.His natural birth no longer has significance.

However, with the older brother, the father was drawing attention away from the state of the relationship to the foundation upon which it was based.

The older brother viewed his relationship with his father in terms of performance. The father's focus was on the genetic bond. The fathe saw him as a son, not because of obedience, but because of birth, not because of service but because of a seed.

The Basis for Our Sonship

Child of God, you are not a son or daughter because of your faithful service, but because you were born of God's seed. You did not qualify to be a child of God by what you did, but have received the nature of a son and daughter by the new birth.

"Whoever has been born of God does not sin, for His seed [Greek, "sperma"] remains in him."

1 John 3:9

"Having been born again, not of corruptible seed but incorruptible, through the word of God which lives and abides forever."

1 Peter 1:23

"But as many as received Him, to them He gave the right to become children of God, to those who believe in His name: who were born, not of blood [natural birth], nor of the will of man [human initiative, power or ability], but of God."

John 1:12-13

The same word *sperma* is used in Greek for the sperm of conception and for the seed of the word of God. Like the son in the story, our right to the position of a son does not come through our own performance or ability. It is established by the fundamental truth of the gospel that God has begotten us as sons and daughters by His *"seed,"* which is His Word.

The accuser of the brethren is intent on convincing you that you have disqualified yourself from the blessings and benefits of being a son and from the joy of intimate fellowship with the Father because of your failure to live up to an impossible standard of perfection. It is imperative that you arm yourself against him with the word of God in your mouth.

Confessing Your Identity As a Son or Daughter

As in the case with healing, it is vital to your victory that you never ever vary your confession of the truth of what God says about you, even though your conduct might be far from fitting for a son of God. It is not your conduct that determines your sonship but your sonship that shapes and governs your conduct. I must declare: "I am a son. God has made me a son. By the new birth I am a son. I have my Father's nature and character because His sperm, His seed *"remains"*(Greek: present tense, continuous action) in me. For that reason I do not continue in deliberate, habitual sin. Because I am a son, He has sent the Holy Spirit to me to guarantee my sonship and my inheritance, and to express the Father's nature in my daily behavior. Now, by the Holy Spirit indwelling me, I can cry out with confidence, 'Abba, Father!'"

The father said to his elder son: *"Son, you are always with me"* (Luke 15: 31). This is the most sublime statement of our position as sons and daughters of God. We are ALWAYS with Him. Our birthright is uninterrupted fellowship and intimacy with the Father.

What About Sin?

I hear a gasp coming from some readers. "But," they splutter, "doesn't sin interrupt fellowship with God? We have heard many preachers say that. Surely God cannot tolerate sin in His presence!"

Yes, that is so. But do you remember the robe? I am clothed with the robe of His righteousness. I do not have the right to intimate fellowship with the Father based on my good works but because He has declared me to be righteous through my believing in Jesus Christ. Therefore, God does not see my failures, disobedience and sin. He sees His robe. His own righteousness covers me at the expense of Jesus' blood. What a wonderful truth! Hallelujah!

The Privilege of Knowing the Deep Things of the Father's Heart

Let me remind you again of verses that we studied in chapters two and three. In chapter two, we studied John 8:35: *"A slave does not abide in the house forever, but a son abides forever."* We saw there the temporary and fragile nature of the servant's relationship to his master. In contrast to that, we saw the son's security in his position and identity as a son based on his birth into the family. In chapter three, we proceeded to study John 15:15 and discovered Jesus changing the position of the disciples from being servants to being friends, or covenant partners. Jesus described the chief characteristic of this new position in this way: *"**All things** that I heard from My Father I have made known to you."*

What a glorious opportunity was squandered by the older brother. He was always with his father geographically and physically, but obviously never with him emotionally. Had he spent those available hours in intimate conversation with his father, he would no doubt have come to know his father's heart and would have received a revelation of his own position as a son.

My Own Frustration

In the early days of my spiritual journey, I spent many hours reading the Bible and in prayer. I was so diligent in the disciplining of my life to have my daily devotional time with God. Here is the tragedy. I was spending time with Him but, as with the older brother, I was never with Him. My daily quiet time was a performance, a work of self-righteousness.

I was just like the Jewish nation who were ignorant of God's righteousness revealed in the Gospel (see Romans 1:16) and were *"seeking to establish their own righteousness"* (Romans 10:3). I longed for an assurance of uninterrupted intimacy, but because I was so focused on my performance, I never felt that I had done enough to earn that joyous fellowship. Instead of discovering the true nature of God as Jesus revealed Him, all I could see was His awesome holiness exposing my own imperfection.

It took the revelation by the Holy Spirit of the truths shared in this book to open my eyes to the Father's loving kindness and tender mercy. Thank God for the glorious liberty from being a servant that came to me and catapulted me into the exciting adventure of being a son.

My Breakthrough Into Revelation

With that transformation, came the accompanying

release of revelation. When I preach in our home-
land, South Africa, people who knew me before and
heard me preach in my "servant" days are amazed. I
am often asked, "From where do you get all the revelation of the word that flows out of your preaching?"
The answer is simple. The moment I stopped being
a servant and received the Spirit of adoption, who is
also the Spirit of revelation, I began to know the deep
things of God. He began to reveal His true nature to
me.

My precious friend, there awaits you a place of
intimate fellowship that I know you long for and that
is already yours! Do not make the same mistake as
the older brother. Do not spend your entire life learning about God but never knowing Him. If you try to
know Him at a distance, you will be offended by His
actions. They are not always fair. Why? Because
He is merciful, and *"mercy is superior to justice"*
(James 2:13).

Knowing God's Ways

You must know His *"ways"* as distinct from His *"acts"*
(Psalm 103:7). The only way that you will come to
know His ways is when you know His heart. Listen
to David's request: *"Show me your ways, O Lord;
teach me your paths"* (Psalm 25:4). God complied,
and David discovered: *"All the paths of the Lord are
mercy and truth"* (Verse 10).

The reason for the older brother's anger, confusion and whining was that he had never discovered the ways of his father. His hostility to his younger brother (he did not say "my brother" or use his name, but called him *"this son of yours"* (verse 30), and his criticism of his father's actions, reveal his abysmal ignorance of his father's heart, from which these actions had sprung. He had never made use of his father's availability to him to press in and share intimately with his daddy. For this reason, he had never come to know his father's heart and so did not understand his ways. To his performance-orientated mind, his father's ways were unjust and unfair.

It is so easy for us to be offended at some of the things God does. He is merciful and His ways are mercy and truth. They are not always fair! Determine today that you will no longer forego your wonderful privilege of pressing into intimate fellowship with your Father. He longs to reveal the deep things of His heart to you. When you know your Father's heart, then you will know the extravagance of His love and the generosity of His covenant endowments lavished on you. That is your birthright!

CHAPTER 12

The Birthright of Sons: Inheritance

"And he said to him, 'Son, you are always with me, and all that I have is yours.'"　　　Luke 15:31

"Blessed be the God and Father of our Lord Jesus Christ, who has blessed us with every spiritual blessing in heavenly places in Christ."

Ephesians 1:3

"Therefore you are no longer a slave but a son, and if a son, then an heir of God through Christ."

Galatians 4:7

As a child growing up, I won many prizes for Bible memorization and scripture knowledge. I was very proud of my knowledge of Bible facts and trivia. When I turned 13, I was at last old enough to attend a monthly Saturday night Youth for Christ "Squash," a youth gathering held at a local restaurant. On one such Saturday night, the program included a Bible quiz modeled after a popular radio program in South Africa, called "Pick-a-Box."

I can remember now, nearly forty years later, the excitement that I felt when my name was drawn to be a contestant. Since it was a Bible quiz, I felt pretty confident in my ability to ace the questions, which would then allow me into the bartering stage, called "The money or the box." The boxes would contain some good prizes but most contained what we called "booby prizes." The oft-repeated slogan of the radio show was: "Remember, there are more big prizes than booby prizes." The disappointment of many contestants who had traded away large sums of money to keep the box which, when opened, had some worthless trinket in it, caused me to doubt the veracity of that statement.

On this particular night, having answered all the previous questions perfectly, I now faced the last question. If I answered this one correctly, I would be permitted to go through to the exciting stage of nail-biting decision as to whether to take my chance on the box I had picked, or to settle for the money being offered by the host. This was the last question that I had to answer: "What is the root of all evil?" I did not have to think twice about the answer. Quickly I blurted out, "Money!"

I can distinctly remember the awful feeling of confusion, followed by self-justification, followed by acute embarrassment when the host "gonged" me out. Then he gave the correct answer: "The love of money." I don't believe that I will ever forget that truth. The high cost of learning it has indelibly marked it in my conscious mind. Money is not the problem, but rather, the love of it.

The Big Deception

Poverty is one of the greatest curses that have de-
scended on the human race through Adam's sin. What
has made it even more entrenched in the entire
world is its connection to religion. The legalistic,
religious system in which I was raised elevated poverty to the stature of a virtue. No wonder I messed
up on my answer! I grew up believing that a truly
spiritual person would be poor. We had an innate
suspicion of anyone who had wealth. Money was the
root of all evil, as far as I was concerned.

As I look back now, I am amazed at how scriptures were so frequently distorted to support such
a Biblically inaccurate religious position. Scriptures that seemed to imply material wealth were
quickly qualified as referring only to spiritual
wealth.

One of the greatest distortions that I grew up
believing was that to be like Jesus was to be poor.
That is a lie repeated often enough until some who
are blessed materially, feel less spiritual and under
pressure to hide their blessing or to give it away.
What is the Biblical truth about poverty and
prosperity?

A Brief Biblical Foundation for Prosperity

1. Jesus' poverty was temporary and had a redemptive, substitutionary purpose.

"For you know the grace of our Lord Jesus Christ, that though He was rich, yet for your sakes He became poor, that you through His poverty might become rich."   2 Corinthians 8:9

He became poor on the cross just as he became sin for us. Our focus should not be on His poverty but on our wealth! To reject wealth and prosperity is to insult the grace of our Lord Jesus! Is He still poor? No! He has been restored, with higher honor than ever before, to the glory and wealth that he had with the Father.

2. We are not to be like Jesus in the form of life that He lived while He was on this earth.

"Because as He is, so are we in this world."
1 John 4:17

Notice that John does not say, *"As He was,"* indicating His time on the earth. He says, *"As He is."* If Jesus is poor now then poverty is what we should embrace. The idea is utterly preposterous! There is no poverty or lack in heaven. Therefore we should not be living in poverty either.

3. According to Isaiah 61:1, the first area that the anointing deals with is poverty. Why would poverty be placed at the top of the list of Jesus' ministry? For a couple of reasons:
   a. Poverty, lack and deprivation were some of the first effects of the curse of Adam's sin. Adam and Eve were cast out of the paradise of plenty to survive by the sweat of their brow.
   b. A person, who is under a yoke of poverty, has difficulty receiving. Some of the effects of poverty are self-sufficiency, pride and unworthiness. All of these will keep that person from being able to receive all of the blessings and benefits that the Anointed One desires to bring them.
4. Since we are Abraham's seed, we have the same covenant call that was given to Abraham. God promised him:

"I will bless you...and make you a blessing...in you all the families of the earth shall be blessed." (Genesis 12:2-3)

God recognizes that in order to bless others, you first have to be blessed. He therefore promises you all the resources that you need in order to be a blessing:

"And God is able to make all grace abound

toward you, that you, always having all sufficiency in all things, may have an abundance for every good work. " 2 Corinthians 9:8

Poverty is one of the greatest manifestations of self-ishness that any one can demonstrate. Since God called you to bless all the families of the Earth, for you not to receive the riches that Christ purchased for you is an act of supreme selfishness.

All That I Have Is Yours

Having laid this brief Biblical foundation, let us now go back to the father's words to his son:

"Son, you are always with me, and all that I have is yours. "

Luke 15:31

We have already seen why the son could not receive what was rightfully his. His servant mentality was the blockage. In the same way, so many of God's children are unable to receive what is rightfully theirs by covenant. God says to us: *"All that I have is yours. "* Looking at so many Christians, you would think that God is stingy and poor. Not so! It is the religious servant-mentality that is closely related to a spirit of poverty that blocks them from receiving all that is theirs.

Mephibosheth: A dead-dog mentality

Mephibosheth, an Old Testament character best il-
lustrates this. Mephibosheth was the son of Jonathan
and the grandson of King Saul. Since a covenant had
been made between David and Jonathan,
Mephibosheth was the heir of the covenant promises made by David to his beloved friend.

There came a day when David summoned
Mephibosheth to His palace and fulfilled his covenantal obligation:

> *"Do not fear, for I will surely show you kindness for
> Jonathan you father's sake, and will restore to you
> all the land of Saul your grandfather; and you shall
> eat bread at my table continually."*
>
> 2 Samuel 9:7

Notice the parallel between David's declaration and
that of the father in the two stories we are studying.
Both are a promise of intimacy and inheritance, of
position and possessions. Mephibosheth was to eat
bread at David's table *"continually."* That parallels
the father's words: *"You are always with me"* (Luke
15:31). David restored to mephiboshefh *"all the
land"* that had belonged to his grandfather, and the
father said, *"All that I have is yours."* The son's
birthright was the same as Mephibosheth's covenant
rights: intimacy and inheritance.

The story of Mephibosheth is tragic. Although he was received and enriched by David through the covenant, and though he sat in the king's palace among David's sons enjoying the bounty of David's table, his mind was never healed of its self-degradation and the shame caused by his crippled condition. He never changed from seeing himself as a worthless, undeserving *"dead dog"* (Verse 8). That pitiful self-image was the very thing that caused him to ultimately forfeit all of his wealth.

Ziba, Alias Satan

You see, Mephibosheth had a lying, scheming, conniving enemy named Ziba. He was apparently consumed with anger and jealousy toward Mephibosheth. Until David restored the land to Mephibosheth, Ziba, who had been Saul's servant, had treated the land as his own. You can read of Ziba's duplicity in 2 Samuel 16:1-4 and 19:24-30. He was obviously consumed with the desire to get the land back for himself.

The climax to the story is tragic and yet so reflective of many of God's children. When David decided to split the land between Mephibosheth and Ziba, Mephibosheth in an act that I used to consider one of humility, said, *"Rather, let him take it all, inasmuch as my lord the king has come back in peace to his own house"* (2 Samuel 19:30).

It sounds very spiritual for someone to say, "If all I have is Jesus, that is all I need. It doesn't matter if my body is diseased or I am poor. If I have Jesus, then nothing else matters. My kids might be on drugs, my marriage falling apart, but as long as I have Jesus, I am happy."

What is wrong with such thinking? The birthright of the son is not just intimacy but also his inheritance. Mephibosheth's covenant right was to possess his father's inheritance. He forfeited his covenant rights because he was ignorant of the covenant.

It is obvious, from what he said, that he was looking at his own person as the grounds for David's blessing. He never once acknowledged that he was blessed for Jonathan's sake. He did not understand his acceptance and endowment on the basis of covenant. Therefore, since he saw no value in himself, he was ready to forfeit his entire inheritance which was secured for him by his father in the covenant made with David.

The Name: The Key to Covenant Inheritance

In preaching on Mephibosheth, I love to dramatize this climax to the story. I delight to ask an audience this question: "What should Mephibosheth have done when David was splitting his inheritance between him and Ziba?" Think about it for a moment. What should he have done? There are many things that he could have done but, really, there was only one simple thing that he needed to quietly say: "Jonathan! Jonathan! Jonathan! Jonathan!"

The mention of that name would have stopped David in his tracks in the action he was taking. He would have remembered his precious friend whom he loved so deeply. He would have remembered back to the two occasions when, because of their intense love for each other, they had made covenant with each other. He would have remembered the promises he had made to Jonathan and would immediately have had to reverse his decision.

Satan Our Enemy : The Usurper

We, too, have an enemy. His name is Satan. He too has stolen what does not rightfully belong to Him. God gave it to Adam and Eve and their offspring. Satan usurped, through his lying treachery, that which God had placed under man's feet and over which He had given him dominion.

The only way that you can resist the devil is by knowing your rights as a son and standing firmly on them. That will involve the confession of your mouth. You will have to declare the covenant promises of God to you as a son repeatedly and authoritatively. Satan does not want to give up the possessions he has stolen from us and the dominion he has usurped from us. The Bible instructs us:

> *"Resist him, steadfast in the faith."*   1 Peter 5:9

To resist the devil means to stand firm against him. The word translated *'steadfast'* means "firm" or "hard." What is called for is an unyielding and unwavering stance in faith.

Faith is of no benefit in resisting the devil if it remains silent. My faith in the word must become verbal and vocal! We must *"hold fast the confession of our hope without wavering,"* (Hebrews 10:23). The devil will use intimidation, weariness, discouragement and disappointment to stop our confession of what God has said. He does not want us to prosper. He wants to keep us in lack and poverty.

In the Name of Jesus

We, like Mephiboseth, have a covenant name that unlocks the treasure chest of the wealth that is ours by covenant. You can readily understand why the enemy tries to keep our focus on ourselves. As long as we are coming to God based on who we are in ourselves and what we have done, we will slink out of His presence as paupers, crawling out in shame and unworthiness. But when we grasp that our rights and privileges are in the name of the one who

made covenant with God the Father on our behalf, we
will come boldly and expectantly, speaking the name,
"Jesus, Jesus, Jesus!"

Right now begin to confess what Jesus has declared
to us: *"All that I have is yours."* Say right now, "All
that the Father has is mine!"

The enemy will immediately come with his intimidation and will begin to accuse you within your heart,
"Who do you think you are? What right do you have
to come to God so boldly and confidently?"

Declare, "All that the Father has is mine, in the
name of Jesus!"

Don't stop saying that until you begin to walk in
the fulfillment of it and begin be a blessing to all the
families of the earth.

CHAPTER 13

Repenting Out of the Servant's Quarters

"And he said to him, 'Son, you are always with me, and all that I have is yours.'"   Luke 15:31

Like me, you probably grew up having your parents read fairy tales to you. Sometimes there would be a threatening danger in the plot of the story. As children, it was easy for our imaginations to get caught up in the drama of the story so that our emotions would follow the swing of the changing fortunes of the hero or heroine. There was always one comfort. Every story ended well: "And they all lived happily ever after."

Jesus did not give us a conclusive ending to this story. He left it at the point where the older brother was still angry while the party continued to celebrate the return of the prodigal. Although providing an ending of our own may be mere speculation, experience with human nature suggests numerous endings, every one feasible. I like to add a speculative spin of my own to this story. Naturally, it is totally uninspired, but it is, nevertheless, a tragically accurate commentary on so many Christians. Bear with me then as I tell my tale.

The festivities have ended, the servants are engaged in the massive clean up of the dining area. The father sits in his favorite chair. On the one hand he is very happy to have his young son back, but, on the other, he is troubled by the hostility and anger of his older son. He is lost in a reverie as he thinks over the events of this momentous day.

Suddenly, a gnawing thought breaks into his consciousness. He realizes that he has not seen his young son around for a while. He begins to wonder, *Where could he be?*

He beckons to one of the head servants and asks him, "Have you seen my young son anywhere?"

"Yes, sir," replies the servant, "I saw him going out the back of the house in the direction of the servants quarters."

The father hurries out the back door as the sun sets on the horizon. As he makes his way down the path to the servants quarters, he meets another servant hurrying about his duties.

"Have you seen my young boy?" asks the father.

"Yes, sir," replies the servant with a nonplussed look on his face, "I saw him entering one of the rooms down in the servants quarters."

The father quickens his pace as he hurries along down the path, realization beginning to dawn on him. He enters the servant's compound and finds the room where his young son is preparing a place to sleep.

"Son, what are you doing here?" the father asks.

"Preparing a place for myself for the night," replies the son.

"But son, don't you understand that I did not receive you back as a servant but as a son? Come back to the house, back to your room. It's waiting for you."

The young son, with obvious embarrassment, averts his eyes from his father's gaze. He is unable to look into those loving eyes. He replies slowly, "Father, you don't know the evil things that I did in the far country. I am so ashamed of what I have done to bring such dishonor to your name. I feel too ashamed and unworthy to sleep under the same roof as you do."

"Son," replies the father, "Don't you understand what I have done for you? I no longer see you as the son who lived a disgraceful life in a far country. When I called for the servants to place on you the best robe, I was covering all of your old life with the gift of a new life. That robe represents my own life. Your old life is gone, covered by the restored life I have given you. What you did while you were in the far country is now irrelevant since you are not here because of any goodness of your own but because of the new life I have given to you symbolized by the robe you are wearing right now."

"But, Father," insists the son, "you have no idea how terrible the things that I did really were. Your goodness in receiving me back is the very thing that makes what I did in the far country seem to be so terrible. The shame I feel over the life that I lived makes it impossible for me to accept a position as a son. I am completely happy to be a servant in your house for the rest of my life. Your kindness in receiving me back demands that I be content with a position as a servant."

"No, son," the father responds, "that can never be! For me to treat you as a servant would be a complete negation of my act of mercy in receiving you home. For you to continue to think of yourself as a servant would be a total misunderstanding of and a lack of appreciation for my act of mercy in receiving you home as a son."

"Father, believe me," replies the son, "I will be absolutely content with a servant's position and a servant's wages. How could I possibly have any expectations beyond a wage since I have already taken and squandered my inheritance in the far country? I came home to be a servant and that is what I intend to be for the rest of my days. I will serve you faithfully out of gratitude for your kindness in receiving me back."

The father, exasperated over the young son's inability to grasp the significance of his gracious act, responds, "Son, do you not understand that when I gave you my robe, it was a guarantee that everything that I have belongs to you. How can I pay you a wage out of what I have already covenanted to you? It belongs to you as much as it belongs to me!"

"No, Father, I have no right whatsoever to expect anything more than a servant's position and wage."

"Son, the ring on your finger and the sandals on your feet declare otherwise. It is true that you have forfeited your own previous rights as a son. However, when I placed that ring on your finger, I was giving you my own authority. You do have a right to the benefits and blessings of being a son and an heir! I guaranteed that when I gave you my ring."

The young boy turns away from the father whose forceful words have seemed to make absolutely no impression on him. The guilt that he feels and the dark memories that he carries within him have so blinded him that he can see neither the father's mercy nor the grace that has been extended to him.

"Come on home to where you belong, son," the father begs.

"No, Father, that can never be. I will stay here and serve you the rest of my life."

The father turns and dejectedly leaves the servants quarters and returns to his house. Though he often tries to get through to his young son, no amount of reasoning can convince the young man of the significance of what the father did in that amazing moment when he ran to him, threw his arms about him and kissed him. For the rest of his days, the father would grieve over both of his sons who could

never come to know and understand his loving kindness and merciful generosity. He would continually
marvel at their unbelief in not being able to receive
their true positions as sons and enjoy intimacy with
their father and utilize all the riches that belong to
them by inheritance. Both would continue to serve
him faithfully while neglecting their true inheritance of entering into a deep relationship of loving
intimacy with their father.

How We See Ourselves

Little needs to be added to grasp the application of
this possible ending to the story of the Prodigal Son.
Instead of a "happily ever-after" ending, many
Christians are writing a tragic ending to their lives
because of their unbelief, ignorance and rejection
of the Father's mercy and grace. Why is this hap-
pening in so many believer's lives?

I am convinced that the major problem is our inability to see ourselves as God sees us. This has
come about because of our overwhelming self-con-
sciousness formed by our past upbringing and performance. Rather than believing the truth of the
testimony of God's word, we are unable to go beyond the body of evidence from our past that con-
vinces us of our unworthiness and condemns us to
the position of a servant for the rest of our lives.

It is imperative that we allow the truth of God's

word to challenge the deception of Satan who uses our history against us. Listen to what Paul said:

> *"For you are all sons of God through faith in Christ Jesus. For as many of you as were baptized into Christ have put on Christ. There is neither Jew nor Greek, there is neither slave nor free, there is neither male nor female; for you are all one in Christ Jesus. And if you are Christ's, then you are Abraham's seed and heirs according to the promise."*
>
> Galatians 3:26-29

The Greek word for *"put on"* is *enduoo*. It is used for putting on clothes. It is used, for example, in Luke 8: 27 of the demoniac who *"wore"* no clothes. Just as the father gave the young son the best robe, so our Father has given us His best robe, His own righteousness packaged in the person of His own son. Now, says Paul, when I am baptized into Christ, I am clothed with Christ himself. When the Father looks at me, He sees Christ who clothes and envelopes me. So complete is that envelopment, that Paul can say that all natural, visible distinctiveness is totally done away with. *"There is neither Jew nor Greek..."*(Verse 28). God no longer sees me as I once was and as others might persist in seeing me. Nor does God see me as I see myself. Now, since He sees me clothed with Christ who is His righteousness, I have to change the way I see myself. I am a son not a servant. That is how God sees me.

Repentance

The desperate need of the Church is for repentance, not from being in the far country and the pig pen, but from living in the servants quarters. The Greek word for repentance *metanoia* literally means "a change of mind." In the story of the Prodigal Son, the older brother desperately needed to repent. He needed a change of mind from his servant mentality to the reality of being a son. What, again, are the two marks of a son? Firstly, *"you are always with me"* signifying his position of intimacy, and secondly, *"all that I have is yours"* signifying his possessions through inheritance.

Now, the younger brother needed to repent as well. He had come home with the purpose of being hired as a servant: *"Make me like one of your hired servants"* (Luke 15:19). However, his father had received and reinstated him as a son. This confronted him with the challenge of overcoming his mindset of guilt and unworthiness in order to embrace the person whom the father, by his merciful actions, had declared him to be. Would he be able to receive the truth that could set him free? That was the dilemma he faced. He needed to repent, to allow his mind to be changed by the powerful truth that confronted him.

That is the dilemma we also face. On the one hand there is the persistent memory of the past with its failures, hurts and strongholds. On the other hand, there is the revelation of the gospel of God's grace in Christ that shows me who I now am in Christ. In so many of our lives, the voice of condemnation seems to totally drown out the voice of revelation. We then find ourselves in the danger of doing what Romans 8:15 warns us against. We *"receive"* a spirit of servitude *"again"* which leads us into fear as the underlining motivation of our relationship to God. We get back into being a servant instead of being a son.

A Spiritual Problem

What we are dealing with here is not just a wrong mindset caused by ignorance and misinformation but a spiritual problem. We have received a spirit which ensnares us and wars against the truth so that we cannot embrace who God has declared us to be. We need spiritual deliverance from that deceiving, destructive, damning spirit, an emissary of the devil, sent to us to prevent us from entering into our position and possessions as sons and daughters of the Father.

Here is the problem. Spirits do not just go away by themselves. They must be evicted and ejected from dwelling in places that do not belong to them. How does that happen?

Firstly, ignorance is not bliss: it is bondage. Jesus

declared that *"the truth will set you free"* (John 8:32). That is the purpose of this book. My one objective has been to declare truth by the Holy Spirit that you might receive the Spirit of wisdom and revelation who will open the eyes of your hearts (see Ephesians 1:17). No matter how much you might rebuke the spirit of slavery and servitude, if you are not renewed in the spirit of your mind by the truth, you will always go back into bondage.

The truths contained in this book are focused on renewing your mind with biblical truth that will expose the lies that the enemy has used to keep you in bondage. In order to repent, you first must recognize the enemy's lies that have bound you in servitude. That is what you are to repent from. But that is only half of repentance. The other part is to embrace the truth.

I believe that if you have read this far, you are ready to do just that. Before we move into greater detail in the next chapters on how to receive liberty and deliverance, why do you not open your heart wide to the Father and repent in the words of this prayer:

Father,
In the name of Jesus, I repent of my wrong understanding of who you are and who You have declared me to be. I repent of the satanic lies that I have believed that have kept me living in the servants

quarters, trying to earn your favor and waiting for a reward. I ask your forgiveness for not having understood the mercy that you showed me in Christ when you saved me and called me your child. I have allowed the devil to convince me that I am too unworthy to live in your house and sit at your table as a son or daughter. I ask forgiveness for having so lightly esteemed your grace and goodness in choosing to believe the devil rather than You, Father God.

Thank you for the truth that has been transforming my understanding. I now receive your Word. I resist the spirit of seduction that has caused me, like Eve, to believe the enemy rather than my Father. I rebuke the spirit of fear that has dominated my thinking about myself and my relationship to Father God. I rebuke the spirit of bondage, slavery and servitude that has kept me in a performance trap trying to please God and earn His favor and love. I tell these spirits right now to leave me, in the mighty name of Jesus, and never to return.

I receive Your forgiveness and cleansing, Father, and now embrace your truth concerning who I am and my relationship to You. I now receive the Holy Spirit, who is the Spirit of Adoption to come and fill me with the assurance and joy of being a son and not a servant!

Thank you, Father. In Jesus' name,

Amen.

CHAPTER 14

Made Whole

"He saith unto him, 'Wilt thou be made whole?'"
John 5:6, KJV

"I have made a man every whit whole."
John 7:23 KJV

There is a fallacy in much of western Christianity that has kept the church of Jesus Christ in immaturity and bondage. That fallacy is the assumption that if we only could have the right information, we would live gloriously successful Christian lives. Christianity has developed into a rational dogma to be understood and then lived out. We have become "cerebral" rather than "cardiac," with head knowledge rather than heart experience.

Fortunately, the Word of God is not as shallow as our Christianity has become. The truth is always addressed to the *heart* of man which is much more than man's rational mind. The heart involves both the rational and emotional parts of man. A man might understand truth in his mind but if he is broken in his emotions, he will be unable to walk in the truth that he understands.

Heart not Head Revelation

Paul, in his magnificent prayer in Ephesians 1, prayed that *"the eyes of your heart may be enlightened"* (Verse 18, NASB). Both the King James Version and the New King James Version of the Bible follow an alternate Greek text (not as well supported by manuscript evidence) that reads *"understanding."* The best manuscripts, however, have the word *kardias* meaning *"heart."* Paul was praying for a revelation that was deeper than mere intellectual conviction or rational comprehension. He was praying for the inner man to be enlightened.

Comprehension

In a similar way, in Paul's prayer in chapter 3, Paul prayed for the following:

> *"That He would grant you, according to the riches of His glory, to be strengthened with might through His Spirit in the inner man, that Christ may dwell in your hearts by faith; that you...may be able to comprehend...to know the love of Christ which passes knowledge."*   Ephesians 3:16-19

Again, our western mindset fails us miserably in grasping what Paul is praying. To us, *"comprehend"* is a word that involves intellect and reason. The

Greek word that Paul used here, however, is *katalambanoo* which means "to fully receive." This is not mere intellectual understanding. Paul said that this love *"passes knowledge."* He was therefore implying a far deeper activity than mere intellectual comprehension. He was praying for an experiential reality that is accomplished by the Holy Spirit *"in the inner man."*

The great tragedy of present day Christianity is that there has never been a day when the church was as blessed with knowledge, information and accurate interpretation of the Bible. At the same time, we have been remarkably powerless to walk in the truth that we claim to know so well. Could it be that Biblical "knowing" is so much deeper than what we understand knowledge to be? Jesus said: *"And you shall know the truth, and the truth shall make you free,"* (John 8:32). Why then, in this age of expansive information, skillful interpretation and profound instruction in Biblical truth, are so many believers still living in so much bondage?

I am convinced that the answer lies in the prayer quoted above where Paul prays that the Ephesians (and we) would know the love of Christ in a way that *"passes knowledge."* That implies knowing with the entire being, not merely intellectual comprehension and understanding.

"Wilt Thou Be Made Whole?"

We have lived at a superficial level of experience, I
believe, because of the shallow application of the gospel to the individual. In contrast to our superficial-
ity, let me draw your attention to the verses quoted
from John 5 at the beginning of this chapter. Jesus
confronts the man at the pool of Bethesda with this
question: *"Wilt thou be made whole?"* After thirty-
eight years of being paralyzed and hoping for an
angelic miracle, the man is more than physically
crippled. In his response to Jesus it is very easy to
discern rejection, bitterness and a sense of abandonment. This man is in need of mental, emotional,
and spiritual healing, besides the obvious physical
miracle that he has waited for so long.

Now look at Jesus' description of the miracle that
He performed. In John 7:23, in responding to the
criticism of the Jews in the temple, Jesus questions
them: *"Why are you angry with me for healing the
whole man on the Sabbath?"* Jesus uses two different words that can be translated *"whole"* here and
in John 5. The first word *holos* means "entire, complete, every part." The second, *hugios*, means "restored to former state, (e.g. *"as whole as the other"*
Matthew 12:13), sound, free of defect."

It is imperative that once again the Church have its
faith elevated to believe for the transformation that
Jesus ministered to this cripple. We have been so

content to accept partial healing as being the Divine purpose for man. We have interpreted the Scriptures against the backdrop of our powerlessness and, just like the religious leaders of Jesus' day, denuded them of their power. For most Christians, there is no hope of the total freedom and wholeness such as Jesus promises and brings. We have been made to believe that only "in the sweet by-and-by" will we know such a wonderful deliverance.

If we are to see servants becoming sons, we need to recognize that the superficial way in which we have applied the healing power of the gospel to the human condition will always leave people falling short of God's best for them. Jesus made the **whole** man **whole**. The Gospel needs to be applied to the whole man, body, soul and spirit, if we are to take our rightful place as sons.

Healing the Broken Heart

Of special interest to us in this study is the emotional wounding or "broken-heartedness" (to use a more Biblical concept) that afflicts so many Christians today. Those wounds are kernel to the perpetuation of the servant-mentality that afflicts the church of Jesus Christ. God through Isaiah promises us that the anointing which would be upon His Anointed One, Jesus the Son, would heal the broken-hearted, (Isaiah 61:1, Luke 4:18).

A remarkable textual variation in Jesus' reading
from Isaiah 61 as recorded in Luke 4:18 provides
some wonderful insight into both the cause of and
cure for emotional wounds. All the Greek manuscripts of the New Testament available to us record a
phrase which does not occur in the Isaiah passage:

> *"The Spirit of the Lord is upon Me, because He has
> anointed Me to...proclaim...recovery of sight to the
> blind."*

In addition, some later manuscripts record the original phrase *"to heal the broken hearted."* Earlier
and more reliable manuscripts omit this phrase completely. When I first discovered this variance, I
was distressed that such an important aspect of the
ministry of the Anointed One should be omitted from
the better manuscripts. Then, the Holy Spirit began
to give me insight into the significance of Jesus' interpretation of what Isaiah had recorded.

Opening Blind Eyes

Emotional wounding is caused by a child's (or, for
that matter, an adult's) **perception** of events. A
child observes and then records in their memory the
actions and words of a parent or some other person
according to how he or she perceives them. That
perception might not be accurate. Children can

easily misunderstand words and actions for they do
not have the maturity to accurately discern motives
and soundly interpret the events that they are experiencing. Their perception of events, the way they
record them in their memories, might be completely
distorted. Nevertheless, that perception and interpretation of childhood experiences will form the foundation of their personality, their self-worth, their sense
of right and wrong and, particularly, the foundation
of their emotional health. It is for this very reason, I
believe, that Jesus did what He did in the synagogue
in Nazareth in interpreting Isaiah's text.

In order for the broken heart to be healed, sight
must be restored. This would harmonize with Paul's
prayer in Ephesians 1:18 that we have already considered, where Paul asks God for an operation of the
Holy Spirit to open the *"eyes"* of the *"hearts"* of his
readers.

If we are emotionally damaged by our perceptions of events in our lives, is it not logical that healing
for those damaged emotions would come by revelation of truth that transforms our perception of ourselves, our parents, and then, by extension, our perception of the Father? We need our emotional, spiritual and mental sight restored by the Anointed One.
When our eyes are opened, our broken hearts will
be healed.

The Model for the family

The key figure in any child's upbringing is their father. I know that runs contrary to much of our matriarchal-society thinking, but it is Biblically supported. Let me draw your attention again to Paul's prayer:

"For this reason I bow my knees to the Father (the best-supported manuscripts omit "of our Lord Jesus Christ") from whom the whole family in heaven and earth is named.   Ephesians 3: 14-15

The "name" denotes the character. Paul is saying that God is the prototypical Father from whom every family derives its character. If we want to understand how the family should function, we must understand the fatherhood of God. Conver-sely, not understanding in an experiential way who God is as father will always cripple our earthly families.

God's purpose for mankind is that every child should grow up in a family that derives its pattern from God as Father. More precisely, every child should grow up with a father who is a perfect expression and likeness of God asFather.

It is abundantly clear that no matter how wonderful, loving and kind our earthly fathers might be, none of them have ever been able to approach the perfection of the God-model of fathering. No matter how good they may be, we also face the likelihood that there will be times when, in the immaturity of childhood, we will perceive things inaccurately. To the degree, whether greater or lesser, that our own fathers fell short of that mark, whether actually or merely in our perception, to that same degree we are emotionally scarred and need the healing power of the anointing to heal our broken hearts.

Here is our difficulty. Many of us have great difficulty recognizing to what extent we are scarred. Still others have such a sense of intense loyalty to their parents that it is difficult to become honest in assessing our own woundedness and the role of our parents, particularly our fathers, in scarring us. It is easy to live in denial. Others have such intensely painful memories of rejection and/or abuse that the damage and pain seem insurmountable, and they live in hopelessness and despair and see no way of ever changing and becoming well.

Not Blame-Shifting and Accusation

Please understand my purpose and motivation here. I am not interested in the methodology of modern psychology of blame-shifting. Nor am I recommending digging around in your memory and coming up with some "repressed memory" of parental abuse. The Holy Spirit is the *"Spirit of revelation,"* (Ephesians 1:17). This is His work. His purpose is not to bring you to a place of blaming or accusing your father, but to a place where you can forgive the debts (or your perception of the debts) that he owes you for failing to be the father that God intended him to be. His purpose, as the *"Spirit of truth"* is to lead us *"into all truth,"* (John 16:13). His purpose is to make the *"whole"* person *"whole."*

In the last chapter of the book, I will be sharing with you some practical "how to" steps in dealing with the perceptions, memories and hurts from childhood that prevent you from relating to God as Father. But first, I want to share with you my own story and pray that God will use it to help someone come into the wonderful liberty of being a son.

CHAPTER 15

My Bethel

" 'I will arise and go to my father...'
And he arose and came to His father. But when he
was still a great way off, his father saw him and
had compassion, and ran and fell on his neck and
kissed him. "   Luke 15:18,20

I never cease to be amazed at the awesome grace of
God. When I look back over my life, I am overwhelmed at how patiently, mercifully and gener-
ously the Father has dealt with me. Many times,
when I thought that I was initiating a move toward the
Father, I discovered that it was his love and mercy
that was both drawing me and waiting to embrace
me as I came to Him.

I thought that the time of waiting on God in
fasting, study and prayer that I had planned at the
mouth of the Igoda River in January 1982 was
because of my own desire and desperation to be
free. I was to discover that when I arrived there,
Father God was waiting for me. Like Jacob at
Bethel, I was to be surprised by His presence at my
personal Bethel.

I have already referred to a number of things,
both theological and experiential that I received

from my own father that needed to be transformed by
revelation and healing if I was ever to receive God as
the Father He really is. My father was a wonderful
man, mightily used by God, and I know that he genu-
inely loved me. I thank God for him and for the wonderful things that he imparted into my life. I honor
him as my first spiritual mentor and teacher to whom
I owe so much. I look forward to being reunited with
him in heaven and marveling together at the amazing
grace of God to both of us.

Nevertheless, he was the product of his own family, cultural, church and educational upbringing.
Though the grace of God had done its work in him
in many areas, there were others that, in my perception, never reflected the true nature of the Father.

Our family had spent many wonderful times camp-
ing, picnicking and vacationing at Igoda in my earlier years during the time of Daddy's pastorate at
Woodbrook Baptist Church in East London. So many
memories flooded back with an acute clarity as I
opened my heart to truth in that travel-trailer or "cara-
van" as we called it in South Africa. I began to see
so many areas where I had been affected negatively
by Daddy's instruction and example. These became
increasingly apparent as I studied the nature of
God as Father. As I studied the books of Romans and Galatians, revelation of the true nature of the Father and His mercy began to penetrate into my religiously-programmed heart,

bringing understanding, freedom, hope and joy. The more I looked into the face of my heavenly Father, the more I could see the areas where I needed to forgive my earthly father.

There came a day when, before the Lord, I spoke the words of forgiveness to my father as though he was still alive and before me. He had gone home to glory in the summer of 1974. I had so many painful memories of our last time together just weeks before His death when we had exchanged very sharp words. There was so much that I had needed to say to him before his death but pride had not allowed me to humble myself and be honest with him. I had spoken words that I wished I could somehow take back and erase.

I clearly recall the great sense of release that came to me as I honestly faced up to the hurts that I had carried for so many years. I needed to deal thoroughly with my perceptions of him and the way he related to me: his rejection of me, his perfectionism that always made me feel a failure, the performance standard to which I could never measure up, and the anger and exasperation which he had displayed when he punished me. As I released him from judgements of him and cancelled the debts I had held against Him, the heavy weight of condemnation, inferiority and guilt began to lift off of me. As I then asked his and the heavenly Father's forgiveness for my bitterness, resentment and anger toward him, a deep cleansing and release took place.

At the same time, God had been showing me through Matthew 18:34-35 how my failure to forgive, being a denial of God's grace and forgiveness to me, had forced God to hand me over to tormentors. When I have received His grace and forgiveness and then choose to hold resentment and unforgiveness against another, I demonstrate by my action that I choose justice rather than mercy. God is then forced to deal with me in justice rather than in mercy. James puts it in this way: *"Judgement is without mercy to the one who has shown no mercy"* (James 2:13). Jesus declares that judgement as being delivered *"to the tormentors "* (Matthew 18:34). For many years I had been tormented by allergies. A wonderful by-product of this forgiveness was a physical healing from those allergies.

The result of that glorious time of forgiveness and cleansing was a wonderful deliverance from so many patterns of rejection, performance, fear of rejection, fear of failure, condemnation and guilt that had resulted from my perception of my earthly father and which had warped my relationship to my heavenly Father. It was so easy now to resist the devil at the points of previous defeat and know that he had to leave since the ground that he once possessed through my unforgiveness, had now been reclaimed.

The gift of the Holy Spirit

For so many years prior to this I had fasted, prayed and begged God to fill me or baptize me with His Holy Spirit. Now, as I studied, I began to see that the gift of the Spirit was now available to me since I could now come as a son. The Holy Spirit showed me so clearly that if the Father had answered my prayers before this, I would have received *"by the works of the law"* and not *"by the hearing of faith"* (Galatians 3:2). God had not been able to answer my pleas before this time because I had always asked on the basis of my performance of restitution and repentance and my good works. The Father could not reward my seeking, fasting, praying and begging with the gift that already belonged to me as a promised inheritance. I could only receive the promise of the Holy Spirit as I came with the simplicity of faith as a son convinced that a loving, merciful Father would never refuse me what He had promised me.

Intimacy Restored

Finally, the day came when I had come to the place of receiving in simple faith. The Holy Spirit led me to meet with a pastor in the city who ministered to me with such wisdom and love. That evening, rather

than returning to Igoda, I decided to stay in the city
with Bev and the children. The children had gone
to bed early. Bev had taken her bath and gone to
bed. I came into our bedroom and was overwhelmed
with a desire to pray. As Bev lay in bed, I knelt at
the bedside next to her and began to pray.

Even now as I write I can clearly recall the excitement that I felt as I began to pray. It was as
though I was listening to another person praying.
For the very first time in my life I felt as though I
was right in the Father's presence. No longer was I
a stepchild in the family. No longer was I an outsider longingly looking into a picture of true family
intimacy reserved for others. There was such a sense
of intimacy and communion as words of worship and
adoration poured from my heart through my lips to
Him.

What joy! Never had I experienced prayer like
this. It had always been a discipline, a chore, a duty
and a means of gaining approval. Now it was a delight to be in my Father's presence and talk to Him
so intimately as though He was right there with me.
No longer was there a distance between us.

I have never been the same since that day. Never
again have I had a moment's doubt as to my position
and possessions as a son. The spirit of slavery and
fear, whose oppression I had so long lived under,
had been evicted by the entrance of the *"Spirit
of adoption"*, the precious Holy Spirit. It is

hard for me to exaggerate the dynamic change in
my emotions. Having lived under a spirit of condemnation with its accompanying feelings of unworthiness, abandonment and frustration for so long, the
emotional joy and peace of feeling loved and accepted
was indescribably wonderful.

Joy Unspeakable and Full of Glory

In the years immediately preceding this cataclysmic
change, I had preached through the book of 1 Peter.
When I came to verse eight of chapter one, I was
stymied:

> *"Whom having not seen you love. Though now you do
> not see Him, yet believing, you rejoice with **joy
> unspeakable** and full of glory."*

I was not able to preach on that verse for weeks. It
would have been hypocritical for me to preach something that was not a reality to me. I was sure of one
thing, I had no experiential knowledge of *"joy unspeakable."* For weeks I wrestled with my own joy-
lessness and frustration. Finally, so as not to lose
face with the congregation, I preached a superficial
message on a joy I did not know to people who
obviously did not believe me.

But now, what joy! Oh, glory! Words cannot
describe that joy that is ours by the Holy Spirit. In

fact that is what the kingdom of God is all about:
"Righteousness and peace and joy in the Holy Spirit"
(Romans 14:17).

Beloved, that is your birthright as a child of God.
Do not settle for anything less. Do you remember
Ziba? Your enemy does not want you to have what
rightfully belongs to you. He will fight you with
false accusation, hopelessness, discouragement and
every negative weapon possible to keep you from
living in the intimacy of the Father's house, enjoying the bounty of His table and possessing your promised inheritance. It is time for you to get angry and
violent against the devil. He **must** be resisted. He
will not leave you alone by ignoring him. These
truths that I have been sharing are your spiritual
weapons to use against him to quench the fiery darts
of his lies, condemnation and intimidation.

*"You **shall** know the truth and the truth **shall** make
you free."*

John 8:32

CHAPTER 16

Receiving the Spirit of Adoption

"For you did not receive the spirit of bondage again to fear, but you received the Spirit of adoption by Whom we cry out, 'Abba, Father.' The Spirit Himself bears witness with our spirit that we are the children of God, and if children, then heirs – heirs of God and joint heirs with Christ."

Romans 8:15-17

I have always been leery of books that offer steps, secrets and keys to some cataclysmic spiritual experience that will revolutionize the reader's life, but now I run the risk of doing what I have been critical of in others as I bring this book to a close. What became a wonderful key to my liberation might not work in exactly the same way for you. I am certain, however, of one truth that is universal in application, and I trust that it will become a key to your liberation as well.

Receive

I started out in the first chapter giving you the word that started my journey into sonship. It is the key word to this book and to sonship, and that word is

"receive." I am confident in making such a strong assertion since it is the promise of the word of the Father:

"Much more those who RECEIVE abundance of grace and of the gift of righteousness will reign in life through the one, Jesus Christ."

Romans 5:17

This promise is so wonderful. THE WAY TO REIGN IS TO RECEIVE! That was the revelation that started my glorious journey. If I can but receive the grace and gift of God, I will reign in this life. That is God's promise, not mine.

You might be thinking: "How do I receive? I have tried so hard to believe and receive but it seems impossible?" In the same way that I needed deliverance from spiritual bondage and healing from emotional wounds, you might need a similar removal of the blockage to your being able to receive the Spirit of adoption and, through Him, the Father's abundant grace and gift of righteousness.

In order to be as helpful as I possibly can, I want to give you some practical steps to help guide you through to receiving. But remember, this is the work of the Holy Spirit, not a formula.

Revelation

The journey begins with revelation of truth from the Holy Spirit. This is His work and is not the fruit of your imagination. He will reveal to you:

1. Truth about the Father and your position as a son and daughter which I pray this book has helped to bring you.
2. Truth about yourself and the areas where the Holy Spirit needs to do His mighty inner work.

Recognition

The next step involves identification and recognition, on your part, of those things from the past that have eroded your capacity to trust and receive as a little child and which need to be dealt with in forgiveness, deliverance and healing. This will include memories and damaged emotions that the Holy Spirit will bring to your conscious mind. He will bring these to the surface because He knows that if left unhealed, they will continually block your healing and keep you in defeat. Do not try to conjure anything up.

This is recognition based on the Holy Spirit's revelation, not my visualization or imagination.

Forgiveness

Now you can cancel the debts that are owed to you and that you have been carrying through your life. Be thorough and be specific. Recognize that you are dealing with your perception of events and so this is not a time of accusation but of forgiveness. Place a chair opposite you and picture the person who you need to forgive sitting opposite you in the presence of the Holy Spirit. Use the words that Jesus gave us in Matthew 18:27. *"Loose"* and *"Forgive."* If the one you need to forgive, for example, is your father, speak these words:

> *"In the name of Jesus, I loose you and forgive you all the debt that you owe me and that I have held against you for not being the father to me that I needed you to be. For..."*

Then specifically name each thing that the Holy Spirit has brought to your recognition. Release every debt that the Holy Spirit brings to your memory. Then release your mother, brothers, sisters, or whomever the Spirit prompts you to forgive.

Remember that according to Jesus' teaching in Matthew 18, for forgiveness to be complete, it must be privately communicated to the individual involved. I didn't say it – Jesus did!

A spirit of fear will try to convince you that this is

not necessary and will only cause more trouble. Recognize the voice that makes this suggestion to you for what it is – a spirit of fear. The opposite of fear, according to 2 Timothy 1:7 is a "*sound mind*" which is one that does not question the word of God. If you have any doubts, ask the Holy Spirit to direct you as to the "who, how, when, what and where" of forgiveness.

Deliverance

Take back the ground from the enemy. Unforgiveness has given Him ground in your entire being (see Ephesians 4:27). Forgiveness has now canceled his right to the territory he has occupied. With confidence and authority you can now reclaim that ground. I have dealt with some specific areas in this book and named specific spirits that the Bible names. One of the wonderful manifestations of the Holy Spirit is the discernment of spirits. Ask the Holy Spirit to show you the specific spirits of darkness that have been harassing you. Tell them to leave in Jesus' name. You can use words similar to these:

"*Satan,*
In the name of Jesus, I take back the ground that I have given over to you through bitterness, resentment, anger and unforgiveness. As a redeemed child

of God, I exercise the authority given to me as a son/
daughter of God and tell every spirit assigned to
harass, deceive, intimidate, restrict or oppress me in
any way to go. I tell every one of those spirits
including the spirit of _____ [Name every
spirit that the Holy Spirit within you discerns] to leave
me and never to return.

In the name of Jesus."

Immediately after you have spoken these words,
resisting and expelling the enemy, then invite the
Holy Spirit to occupy every part of your being. Yield
every part of your body to His control, particularly
those areas of your mind and emotions that have been
in bondage to satanic oppression. Do not be surprised if, as you yield to the Spirit and receive His
occupying presence, more areas for forgiveness and
deliverance are exposed.

Healing of the broken heart

Now it is time to open up to the precious Holy Spirit
who, by His anointing, has come to heal your broken
heart. Do not try to dictate to the Holy Spirit what He
should do. This is His work. Your responsibility is to
yield to Him. Do not be in a hurry at this point. Wait
on the Lord. Do not be surprised when he begins to
bring to the surface deep emotions. Jesus taught us a
fundamental truth concerning the Holy Spirit:

"If anyone thirsts, let him come to me and drink. He who believes in me...out of his heart will flow rivers of living water." But this He spoke concerning the Spirit which they that believe on Him should receive," John 7:37-39

The Greek word here translated *"heart"* is *koilias* and means literally "a cavity" and is most frequently translated as "womb." In the King James Version of the Bible, it is translated *"belly."* It denotes the deepest, inward parts of the being. What Jesus is showing us is that receiving the Spirit is not a mere mental assent to some Bible truth. It is profound in its extent and effect. Out of our innermost being, rivers will flow. When the river begins to flow, many times emotional blockages will surface first.

The purpose of this book is not to do an extensive examination of emotional healing. The subject is too important and vast to do it justice in a few sentences. The important thing is this: **trust the Holy Spirit.** He knows what He is doing. Go where He goes as He plumbs the depths of your emotional being. His purpose is healing. He ultimately wants to bring you to *"joy unspeakable,"* joy in the Holy Spirit. I am so thrilled at the wonderful restoration of joy that has been taking place in the Church in this decade! Many are finding deep emotional healing as they yield to the Holy Spirit and allow Him to release rivers of refreshing, healing joy out of their innermost beings. Do not resist His work in your emotions. Simply obey His gracious prompting.

Receiving the Spirit of adoption

This hardly needs to be stated. As you yield to the Holy Spirit and allow Him to do His healing work, he will be removing all the blockages to your receiving. However, one thing does need emphasis at this point. In chapter four, we studied the subject of the *"Spirit of adoption."* It would be good if, at this point you could flip back to that chapter to the section on page 37 headed: "The basis of our acceptance." Note, in particular again, the importance of the confession of your mouth.

It is now time to begin to cry out. Believing that the Father's Word is true and that He has made you a son or daughter, begin to cry out, "Abba! Father!" Cry out loudly and with confidence! Keep crying! Do not listen to the intimidation of the enemy. As you cry the Holy Spirit will set up a duet within as He too, in confirmation, cries out alongside your spirit. In response you will hear the Father replying: *"Son!"*

Wherefore thou art no more a servant, but a son; and if a son, than an heir of God through Christ.

Galatians 4:7

How To Become a Child of God

It is possible that someone who has read this book, has not yet experienced the joy of becoming a child of God. You might be wondering to yourself, *How do I become His child?* God's promise is clear:

"But as many as received Him, to them He gave the right to become children of God, to those who believe in His name."   John 1:12

You become His child by receiving Jesus in a simple act of faith. The best way to do that is in the form of prayer.

Heavenly Father,
I come to you in Jesus' name. Your Word promises that if I receive Jesus, He gives me the right to be your child. I ask Jesus to come into my heart and be Lord of my life. I receive your forgiveness for my sin. Thank You for taking away my sin and making me Your child. According to Your word in Romans 10:9-10, I now confess that Jesus is Lord of my life. I am now Your child!
Your word promises me in Ephesians 1:13 that when I believe in Jesus, you confirm that I am your

child by sealing me with the gift of the Holy Spirit. I now receive the promised gift of the Holy Spirit. Holy Spirit, rise up within me as I confess that I am a child of God. Abba, Father! Abba, Father!

Now begin to praise God for saving you, receiving you, making you His child and filling you with His Holy Spirit. The Holy Spirit wants to give you a special capacity to praise God in a way that transcends the limitation of your intellect, a language that comes from your spirit (see 1 Corinthians 14:15, praying *"with the spirit"*) given to you by the Holy Spirit. Begin to speak those words and syllables that He gives you. You use your voice – He gives the language. Continue to speak out, "Abba, Father." He will respond in your heart with the most wonderful word: "Son!" "Daughter!"